BLACK & BROWN FACES
IN AMERICA'S WILD PLACES

AFRICAN AMERICANS MAKING NATURE &
THE ENVIRONMENT PART OF THEIR EVERYDAY LIVES

BLACK & BROWN FACES
IN AMERICA'S WILD PLACES

PHOTOGRAPHED & WRITTEN BY **DUDLEY EDMONDSON**

Cover and book design by Hilary Harkness
Editors: Brett Ortler, Emily Beaumont

All photos copyright by Dudley Edmondson unless otherwise noted.
Back cover: **Chad Brown** (top)
Interior: **Cheryl Armstrong** (33); **Steve Ash** (184); **Lynnea Atlas** (12);
Elliott Boston III (41); **Chad Brown** (6); **Robert Foxx** (88, 89); **Bill
Gwaltney** (48, 51); **Nancy LatTour-Edmondson** (175); **Mamie Parker**
(104); **Yosemite National Park and the National Park Service** (25)

10 9 8 7 6 5 4 3 2 1
Black & Brown Faces in America's Wild Places
20th Anniversary Edition

First Edition 2006
Second Edition 2025
© 2006 and 2025 by Dudley Edmondson
Published by Adventure Publications
An imprint of AdventureKEEN
310 Garfield Street South
Cambridge, Minnesota 55008
(800) 678-7006
www.adventurepublications.net
All rights reserved
Printed in China
Cataloging-in-Publication Data is on file with the Library of Congress.
ISBN 978-1-64755-586-3 (pbk.); 978-1-64755-587-0 (ebook)

Contents

Foreword

Black & Brown Faces in America's Wild Places represents an important step in countering the exclusion of a significant portion of our country's population from the national wildlife conservation dialogue. The negative repercussions of this exclusion will be hard felt for years to come. We know that people only support what they understand and value. As our nation becomes more culturally diverse, a growing portion of our population is not connected to wildlife and our conservation heritage.

How well we manage and protect our natural resources over the next 100 years will be directly tied to our ability to engage all of our citizens. What draws an individual to want to experience the joy, passion, and fulfillment found in nature? As a wildlife photographer, Dudley Edmondson has asked this question of himself. Perhaps more importantly, Dudley has taken the time and interest to ask this of 19 other individuals who have devoted their lives to wildlife conservation or whose passion is satisfied in wildlife and outdoor recreational activities.

His images and text provide us with the sometimes hidden and somewhat complicated reasons why some find excitement and others find peace in nature. Most importantly, this book illustrates that the job of preserving this incredible resource is too big to turn down anyone's help. We need to identify the incentives and promote wildlife/nature recreation and appreciation among all cultural groups.

No longer can we rely on the programs and strategies used to fund wildlife conservation over the past 100 years—programs that gave us our state and national parks, national wildlife refuges, national forests, and national seashores. Yet as our population grows and places more development pressure on our remaining wild places, sustainable funding for these programs will be more important than ever. Our ability to ensure this funding depends on our ability to help future generations understand, value, and support these natural resources.

For us to have a real impact on the future, we have to influence the next generation. We need to encourage all children to investigate career opportunities in natural resource and wildlife management. Please take this opportunity to introduce the great outdoors to a child you know who may eventually be making key decisions regarding our wild heritage.

We want to thank all of our partners in this project, and especially Dudley for introducing us to these fine people and allowing us to share in their outdoor experiences.

—*James Mallman, President, Watchable Wildlife, Inc.*

Preface

The 20 outdoor role models in this book, first published in 2006, are more relevant today than ever before. When this book was released, people of color were a relative rarity in the outdoors, but over time, we have slowly become more frequent visitors to our public lands. I feel we've discovered the mental and physical health benefits of connecting with nature and are now making it a normal part of our daily lives. People of color have always disproportionately had higher levels of stress due to America's never-ending, tense racial climate. And to add yet another source of stress, our public lands and people of color are under assault by an unprecedented, new authoritarian government. Exposure to nature and getting outside can help offset that somewhat for us.

Thankfully, America's population demographics are changing, and white dominance is declining in something called "the Browning of America." This decline will likely result in people of color (i.e., people of the Global Majority) gaining significant political and economic power, as well as being tasked with continuing the conservation work of our white allies.

The Browning of America has been in full swing since 2013, when for the first time ever, there were more children of color being born in America than white children. That trend is well over a decade old now, and today white children under the age of 18 are considered a minority in this country. The Brookings Institute studies suggest that youth of color will comprise the vast majority of this nation's population growth over the next 40 years.

The reality is that this demographic shift is nothing more than the continued expansion of an already dominant population of people of color who currently make up 85% of the total world population. At no point in human history have people of European ancestry been globally dominant from a population standpoint, so what's happening in America is really the natural progression of an inevitable demographic change arriving in the United States. Needless to say, the Browning of America has a lot of white Americans concerned about the future.

In my mind, this explains the unprecedented assault on women's reproductive rights; aggressive immigration reform policies; and the removal of diversity, equity, and inclusiveness initiatives, as well as efforts to erase Black and Brown history from educational institutions and ban books written by BIPOC authors in libraries around the country.

Nonetheless, there is no doubt that the future America will consist of a browner, more diverse population of people. This should not be seen as negative for white Americans, but an opportunity to work alongside a new generation of Americans who will be responsible for upholding many of the conservation practices and policies that have protected our public lands for generations. But it is also an educational opportunity, to learn from these up-and-coming leaders. People of the Global Majority have traditionally viewed nature in a much different way, one that transcends commodification and extraction. This is counter to the common Eurocentric way of viewing nature.

Lastly, it's an opportunity to understand the critical role that urban green spaces and diverse representatives of nature and the outdoors will play in this new age. About 80% of Americans, including the vast majority of people of color, live in cities. Urban green spaces need to be protected and increased, as they are the first point of contact for urbanites of all backgrounds to understand nature and the impact their actions have on the environment.

How can we expect people to care about our public lands if they have no relationship with green spaces in their own communities? Getting away from the false narrative that nature only exists in faraway, pristine places is a must if we ever hope to solve our environmental problems. Including urban green space in environmental protection plans will help everyone to understand the importance of all of nature for generations to come.

These 20 interviews remain relevant and important today, and I hope they continue to inspire current and future generations to appreciate, enjoy, and protect the environment and the outdoors.

—*Dudley Edmondson*

MY HUSBAND AND I CHOSE TO SELL OUR CAR when we moved to Denver. We feel if a person has an option, they should not drive long distances to work. Part of that is a green decision and part of it is a social decision. I really feel that if people are not willing to live where they work, then they should give the job to someone who is willing to live there.

I think a lot of that comes from the neighborhood where we grew up. My husband and I are both from the same neighborhood in north Minneapolis. It is called Homewood, and in that area a lot of companies that do good business hire folks from the neighborhood. That was true with the school in our neighborhood. When I was growing up, the teachers lived near us. Today, the teachers live as far away as possible.

The environmental benefit is that it does cut down on greenhouse gas emissions, and the other part is a quality-of-life benefit. If I get my workout each day by riding my bike to work or walking to work, then I am a much healthier person than I was when I had a car. Why drive my car to the gym to work out? Even if you are taking the bus or some other mass transit to work, you are a much healthier person because you are walking to the station or bus stop each morning. Most people want to park as close as they can to their job before they walk.

I also see it as a social decision to strengthen community integrity. I have a sense of that as a result of the neighborhood I grew up in. We had Black people, Brown people, white people living together, dedicated to each other and dedicated to providing a high-quality urban lifestyle for everyone in the neighborhood. It did not matter what income level you came from. We

LYNNEA ATLAS

Outdoor Adventure Center Coordinator, Auraria Campus, University of Colorado Denver, Colorado

had teachers and architects in the neighborhood, and a few doctors and people like that, but most of it was blue-collar working-class families. We all wanted the same standard of living, so it worked.

Where I come from, making life choices based on quality of life is not weird. It was the culture of the neighborhood, and it was the norm. The more normal we think it is, the more normal it will become. There are still families raising children there, having similar experiences as I did. Instead of thinking of it as a really unique place, I want to think of it as the start of what our country has to move towards and what our communities have to move towards to thrive.

Childhood Experiences and Turning Points in Nature

A lot of families in our neighborhood took vacations together—groups of adults and kids from all different ethnic backgrounds, Black, white, Latino—traveling around the country. One time a group of families got

Lynnea with her dad

together and went to the Black Hills in South Dakota and went to a ranch for vacation. And yeah, we got crazy looks from people trying to figure us out. I was kind of young and did not notice the stares as much as my folks did. Our parents felt that quality of life and values were far more important than trying to fit into the norm.

I have been participating in outdoor activities since conception, as far as I am concerned. I always joked that I was probably conceived in a tent in the woods somewhere. I can't even tell you when I started, I just remember always being in the outdoors. When I started to do stuff like hiking and cross-country skiing, I was so young my skis were probably about a foot and half long.

What I Do in the Outdoors

I work for the University of Colorado Outdoor Adventure Center on the Auraria Campus in Denver. We serve the university and two colleges, the Metro State College of Denver and the Community College of Denver.

We are a really unique and interesting campus in that we are a commuter campus with no residential housing at all. Our median age for the campus is about 25, so we are also really nontraditional in the context of student age. I am the coordinator for the Adventure Leadership Program.

I just moved to Denver from Minnesota two years ago. I came here to go back to school. Prior to that, I worked about seven and half years for the Minnesota Minority Education Program Partnership, which was a great job working on my passion, increasing academic success for students of color. It is still one of my main focuses, and now I am blessed to be able to put my recreational passion together with increasing success for students.

I also now have the opportunity to help diversify the Outdoor Adventure Program by providing programming that appeals to a wide variety of interests as well a having a staff that is more representative of a diverse population. I have the great support of a department that wants to do those kinds of things at the college level, which feels unique because I don't know of many college programs that measure their success based on how diverse the groups they take into the outdoors are, or how diverse their staff is.

We spend a lot of time developing communications to help people understand the value of experiential education. That is what we do on a daily basis: We provide leadership training and diversity retreats in the outdoors where people are put into situations where they have to experience diversity, not just talk about it in an academic setting.

We go to places like the Rocky Mountains or nearby Utah—as long as it is some kind of natural environment that gives people a chance to get to know one another without all the pretenses and the pressures that society places on us daily about how different we are as individuals.

Heroes and Mentors

My parents are my heroes and mentors, and they are also the people who got me into the outdoors. I would not have the confidence and the knowledge about the outdoors had my parents not been involved in it. They are both avid outdoors people, and in particular my father. He really taught me the basis of what I know about the outdoors. He was a motivator for me; he kept me trying different stuff. He did some stuff that I don't know that I would do even today, like take a Grumman canoe down through the rapids on the Devil Track River in northern Minnesota over a 10-foot waterfall— not me. It sounds crazy to me, but I admire him for his craziness and sense of adventure. It was very encouraging to me.

Even before I could walk, I can remember being in a pack on my father's back while he was hiking or cross-country skiing or snowshoeing. My father is a pretty big, very strong man, with a very, very dark complexion. Oftentimes people see him and are immediately intimidated. But once the "Minnesota nice" comes out, he puts people at ease. He has such a beautiful smile. I have been in some crazy locations in which I know everyone around us was intimidated by him, and he leaves those places having made new best friends.

My current supervisor and director of the Outdoor Adventure Program is a very accomplished desert rock climber and good at pretty much every other outdoor sport, like most Colorado residents. He gave me an opportunity to take my mostly informal training in the outdoors and build those skills and adapt them into outdoor experiential learning. I really look up to my program director as a white person who is dedicated to the quality that culturally diverse environments bring. He puts his money where his mouth is, and that is all I ask of people. No one has all the right answers, but people who are willing to struggle with it and make it happen are everybody's heroes.

Minorities in Our Wild Places

The raw reality is we cannot turn back the clock on the diversification of this country. It is a sink-or-swim kind of situation. People of color are here to stay. Federal and state agencies for environmental protection need to step up and get in the game. They need to let people of color know these places are open to them, that they are welcome, and that they want them to visit. It absolutely has to be inviting. It can't just be "we are nice enough." You have to be welcoming and make people feel like they have a space and that they belong.

In the process, they need to partner themselves with community organizations. For example, if a national park is located on or near tribal lands, then make sure tribal members are the rangers in these parks. People of color want to see other people of color doing stuff in the outdoors. That is a great tactic for drawing in visitors of color to an area.

Youth and Wilderness

I think it is really important for people, regardless of their background, to have experiences that challenge them, that are constantly new to them, that are unique and educational. Wilderness experiences offer all of the above.

Lots of great programs, for years, have been taking urban youths into the outdoors. There have been lots of great success stories that have come from programs like Outward Bound, Wilderness Canoe Base, and some of the YMCA and YWCA programs. The focus of this, however, needs to be changed to where families of color can do these things together, teaching both the kids and parents outdoor skills, so that it becomes a sustainable experience and not just a one-week thing.

The raw reality is we cannot turn back the clock on the diversification of this country.

Best Outdoor Experiences and Favorite Places

My favorite outdoor activity is sea kayaking in Lake Superior back in Minnesota. I was an avid downhill skier in Minnesota, but here in Colorado I am a hard-core snowboarder. If I had no brains at all, I guess I would give up everything in life and just spend all my time in the mountains snowboarding.

I especially love the Boundary Waters Canoe Area of northern Minnesota. It is one of the very few places in this country where you can go and not even see a plane for days, or a telephone pole, let alone another human being, depending on the time of year you are there. There is something very unique about that experience that quiets your spirit enough so that you can look at life with a very fresh set of eyes.

I once spent two weeks during the winter at Adventurous Christians camp in northern Minnesota. Most of that time was spent by myself, supporting the camp, while the owners were on vacation. I would have days when my only company was a group of playful, energetic sled dogs, so I talked to those dogs a lot. I read a lot of books, and I also got really, really quiet. For me, being an extrovert, it was a huge challenge to be alone for two weeks. In that time, I learned the real beauty of winter in the Northwoods—the beauty of a full moon reflecting off the snow at night, or skiing in the early morning over fresh snow.

Being a Face of Color in Remote Places

For African Americans, the key to having the opportunity to experience nature is to be able to do so in a place they feel safe and welcomed. People know they are welcome in big cities and would not hesitate to visit them,

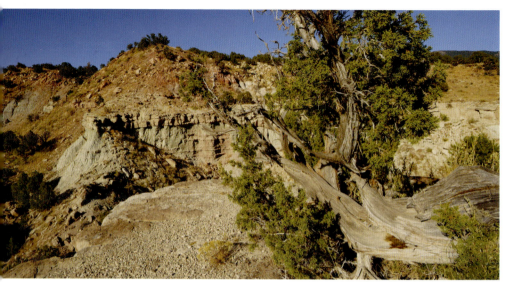
Garden Park near Cañon City, Colorado

but smaller towns are a different story. I do think twice about passing through small towns. I want to know what to expect there. Sometimes that can be very stressful if you are not sure. So the more the stories get out about where you can go and feel welcome, the more people will go there.

I have definitely had experiences here in Colorado where I have not been welcome. Then there have been many places where I have been very welcomed. Ouray, Colorado, and Moab, Utah, are two places in which the people were extremely nice. These are places that I have always felt really welcome each time I go, and I will continue to spend my money in those towns when I travel. Snow Mountain Ranch, YMCA of the Rockies, is another location in which I have always felt welcome. There are a couple of towns here in Colorado, and I won't mention them by name, that I will never visit or spend money in again.

I like going to places around the country where people treat you like a decent, normal human being and are not amazed that a Black person actually left the urban environment and is here in the outdoors. Some of these people clearly have never met or spoken at length with a person of color, and they oftentimes give away that fact by the things they say or the questions they ask. Don't be surprised, just be nice.

If I have one more park ranger aggressively approach me reminding me of "leave no trace" practices, I might just throw up! I know they may mean well, but really, it is not necessary, *really*.

Environmental Advocacy and the Future

The question of environmental pollution as it pertains to people of color and low-income people is a very real issue. These groups of people are often the victims of environmental poisoning, across almost every major city in the country.

People in many cases are working so hard just to keep their heads above water and meet their families' needs, that it is kind of hard to expect them to have time to be environmentalists, even for their own benefit. You're adding insult to injury when you put poor families in highly toxic environments, then expect them to better themselves when you have now added health problems such as asthma to their burden. That is just not realistic.

City government must be held responsible for what they subject low-income residents to; there are just no two ways about it. Cities and states should have a standard of living that they want all people to have, and that should become a priority.

I think it is really important that institutions like the National Park Service, state parks, and the Bureau of Land Management start struggling with the hard problems of how they are going to maintain natural areas when the country's demographics are changing away from a white majority, which has traditionally been on the front lines of environmental protection. There are a lot of barriers, both language and cultural, with which they will have to struggle.

Lynnea and I have been friends since we first met during this book project almost 20 years ago. She now lives in Minneapolis with her son, Bear, and partner, Matt. She is still doing amazing community-building work for outdoor recreation and access, both in her role as Chief Operating Officer of the Girl Scouts River Valleys and as a guide in her free time. Lynnea has spent much of her life championing the outdoors and the need for people of color to be seen as part of those spaces, as policymakers, and as employees of agencies that care for and manage our outdoor spaces. It is very affirming to see that Lynnea is still doing this much-needed work.

—*Dudley Edmondson*

Afternoon folks, my name is Elizy Boman, and I'm a soldier with the 9th Calvary of the U.S. Army. Natives call us Buffalo Soldiers, and I've been assigned to these here parts by the U.S. government to keep folks from misusing these federally protected lands. I tell you, local folks come up here tryin' to graze their live-stock and steal timber, and sometimes there just ain't no easy way tellin' a fella he can't do that. It's a hard pill for these white folks to swallow, havin' colored soldiers telling them what they can and can't do. My regiment rode for14 days from San Francisco at the Presidio to get here. I tell ya, it's nice duty if you can get it. The air here is so cool and fresh, and timber so tall just makes a man happy to be alive.

YOU KNOW YOU HAVE BEEN TALKING TO A GHOST, DON'T YOU? Because soldiers like Elizy have not been in the park since 1904. But the important thing is that Black soldiers like him were here protecting the park before the Park Service was in existence. I am a park ranger here in Yosemite National Park, and I interpret the park's natural and cultural history through the soldier character Elizy Boman, doing my natu-ralist program in full Spanish-American War period uniform. Buffalo Soldiers were here in the park in 1899, 1903, and 1904.

Many people only know of Buffalo Soldiers' participation in the Indian wars, but few know about their role in protecting some of our national parks. There are so few stories of African American stewardship. What I have learned about these soldiers and their lives in the region, protecting parklands, I gathered on my own, with the help of a researcher I hired. Most of the information comes from documents found in the National

SHELTON JOHNSON

**Interpretive Ranger, Yosemite National Park
and Buffalo Soldier Historian
El Portal, California**

Archives and personal letters from soldiers to their family members. Sadly, none of this exists in any book, which made my search that much harder.

Childhood Experiences and Turning Points in Nature

I had a great childhood growing up in Detroit. As a kid, I enjoyed watching National Geographic and Audubon specials, and I had always wanted to visit places like Zion or Arches National Parks. My family moved to Detroit after the race riots, in the aftermath of Martin Luther King's assassination.

I think the reason wilderness has always fascinated me as an inner-city kid was because my father was in the military and as a child I lived in Germany for a while. The earliest experience I had of mountains was when I was only 3 or 4 years old. My parents took me up into the Black Forest in Germany. They showed me this area where, during World War II, Hitler had this secret kind of headquarters. I also vividly remember being up in the German Alps, which was an experience that always kind of haunted me, once I got back to the States. Once I got back to Detroit, visions of grand mountains and snow would not leave my mind. I found myself literally and spiritually elevated when I was there, only to discover that Detroit was nearly the complete opposite of that. I just could not put those mountains out of my mind.

In inner-city Detroit, so much of my life as an African American male was already circumscribed in many ways by the outer society. The thought

El Capitan Meadow, Yosemite National Park

that I was supposed to like basketball or be prone to drug use and violence made me somewhat rebellious toward city life, fueling my interests in wild places like mountains and desert, where I could get away from people and their preconceived notions about me.

It is a religion that is not written down and a spirituality that is not in a book, but the process of walking on a trail into wilderness is a process that is similar to being enlightened in some religious faiths.

What I Do in the Outdoors

As an interpretive park ranger at Yosemite National Park, a typical day for me would be working at the Valley visitor center, getting people oriented to what things are available to them while they are in the park. These include canoe trips, hiking trails, or going on a ranger-led tram tour of the park. I give botany, wildlife, and cultural history talks and walks. I have been doing that in Yosemite for about 12 years. I have actually been a park ranger for about 19 years.

It is a great experience to see someone's eyes light up about an aspect of Yosemite's natural or cultural history. It is then that you realize you have made an impact, literally becoming a living bridge between the park and the public, so that people can travel across your words as though they were made of stone, and walk across that bridge into the greater meanings that underlie the national park.

I tend to think of being a park ranger as a calling, as opposed to an occupation. People don't join the Park Service to make a lot of money. They join it because of some kind of personal belief system about human beings and their role in nature, especially in the preservation of the natural world.

For me, being a park ranger is like my childhood dream coming true, having the opportunity to spend my life in the mountains, or in the desert, or wherever I happen to be, just to be in a place where there are not a lot of people but there is a lot of nature around me.

Heroes and Mentors

My heroes and mentors as a young person were from African American history, people like Frederick Douglass and Harriet Tubman, but I was always partial to mountain men like Jim Beckwourth and Edward Rose, and frontiersmen and trappers. I kind of liked the idea of the West and the African Americans that were connected with that history. Even as a kid, I kind of liked the phrase "Buffalo Soldiers," and I was curious as to why they were called that and what they did. Today, my heroes and mentors are anyone who is doing something good. I admire people who are not in it for the money, but trying to make the planet a better place because it is the right thing to do.

The Spirit and Nature

I do not go to church, even though I was raised Lutheran. One reason I like being out in wilderness is because every time I go there it seems to be a perfect substitute for the church experience. It is not Lutheran or Baptist. It's not Buddhist, Islam, or anything. It's just pure and simple nature. It is a spiritual, sacred experience without all the labels. There is no one out there that is going to teach me or tell me the way, or say, "This is the way to worship. This is the path to the mountain." There is only the mountain and the path, and it is up to me to find my own way and learn what it is I need to know. It is a religion that is not written down and a spirituality that is not in a book, but the process of walking on a trail into wilderness is a process that is similar to being enlightened in some religious faiths.

Being in the mountains and being in wilderness serves as a means for me to connect with something that is greater than myself. I think that everyone needs that, and when they don't have that, there is a spiritual vacuum that is created inside them. Now this is just my own feeling, but I think that one of the issues that affects many African Americans is that many of them do not visit wilderness areas, even though a great deal of them do go to church every Sunday. I think that our ancestors in Africa had a connection to the plants and animals around them, as well as the waterways and land features, and they were more than just the names of places and things, but that connection gave them a sense of where they came from, who they were, and where they were going. In this country, we have regained much of what we lost after leaving Africa, but what we still have to regain is that connection with the natural world. I think that is something for which church by itself cannot substitute. In order to have that, you need to go back to West Africa and go on a trek somewhere, or you need to find it right here in America.

Distant view of Half Dome in the high country, Yosemite National Park

Minorities in Our Wild Places

I have always been a lover of wilderness, but from a faraway place, and that faraway place was Detroit. Even though Detroit is a long way from Yosemite—over 2,000 miles—it is actually philosophically and psychologically at a much greater distance. The same is true of Oakland, California, which is just 100 or so miles from Yosemite. If you live in inner-city Oakland, where there are lots of African Americans, then Yosemite might as well be on the dark side of the moon. The psychological distance is so great, that the subject of the outdoors is never a topic of discussion. In Detroit, there were so few people around me who were backpackers or canoeists or hikers—who even talked about wilderness? I don't remember a conversation with an adult that even ventured into the whole realm of wilderness preservation, or the beauty of mountains, or visiting a national park.

I think it is important to state that when African Americans work in parks or wilderness areas, they usually have traveled a much greater distance than Euro-Americans as a result of the psychological distance that they must overcome to get there. That is not always the case, but I think that, culturally, we are so far removed from wilderness that I am sure there are African Americans who live in Phoenix and have never been to the desert, and there are African Americans who live in Miami and have never been to the Everglades, and there are African Americans in Denver who have never been to Rocky Mountain National Park.

I had to find a way to span that psychological distance between the urban culture and wilderness setting to get here. I am an inner-city kid who dreamed of being in Yellowstone National Park, and for that I was labeled as being strange, bizarre, and odd. In my mind, it made no sense for someone to not want to go to Yellowstone.

Best Outdoor Experiences and Favorite Places

Wilderness is not the sort of place you can drive into. It is best hiked into, allowing you to move into it at a pace at which you can understand its meaning and get a sense of what it is about. Going into wilderness too quickly is like gulping down good wine. If you do that, you don't give your palate a chance to savor it and draw out its true flavor, or allow the aroma and bouquet to fill your senses. The same is true with wilderness. You must savor it, feel it, and take it in one vista at a time. The result brings a deeper, more meaningful experience. I think it should be a crime to speed through wilderness areas. I see it all the time, people speeding in a hurry to get through Yosemite. To visit and experience nature, you have to move at nature's speed.

One of my last jobs when I worked in Yellowstone was to deliver the mail in winter. I did the run twice a week. It was 150 miles by snowmobile, round-trip. I would go out in all kinds of weather because, as you know, "the mail always goes through." I had a chance to experience the park months before the park roads reopened to visitors. So when I was out there, frequently I was all by myself in Yellowstone's 2.2 million acres. I would not see any people most of the time, until I delivered the mail on the other end. There would be huge stretches of wilderness where the only thing I would see were bison. You have a lot of time to contemplate the meaning of wilderness when you are driving through it in the middle of a snowstorm, wondering if you are going to make it. That is another thing about wilderness—nature does have an edge, but it also is an excellent place to learn who you are as a person and your strengths and weaknesses.

Being a Face of Color in Remote Places

I think that one of the reasons why African Americans are not visiting wilderness areas is because they feel conspicuous when they are there, along with safety concerns. "Is my family going to be safe from acts of racism here?" Over the years they have heard stories of things happening to people, even though they may have been blown out of proportion from the actual event. The negatives begin to add up and outweigh the positives, and after a while you no longer even see the positives, because if you've never been there, then how do you know what the positives are?

Yes, I have experienced racial prejudice in the outdoors, right here on my job as a ranger. I am an African American in America, so it goes

Buffalo Soldiers in Yosemite National Park

without saying. I have experienced it in cities as well. It is hard to be in any landscape in America and not experience it. I haven't had anything really bad or horrible happen here; I was not dragged off in the woods and someone threw a rope around my neck. All racial prejudice affects you in some way. Just an odd look or comment can affect you. Things have happened, but I have to ask myself, what is it that I am really weighing here? If the experience had affected me that badly, I would not even be working here. So the fact that I have been working wilderness areas since 1984 means the good far outweighs any bad I have experienced.

Bad things could have happened if I had stayed in Detroit, and I know bad things would have happened to me there. I would much rather be in Yosemite, in California, dealing with what might possibly happen, as opposed to what really would happen in a big city.

In my 19 years working as a park ranger, a few things have happened, like the time I once took a family into a cave in Great Basin National Park that identified themselves as Ku Klux Klan members. I dealt with it by telling them, "That is really great! I like people who stick together!" I said, "Sticking together is really important here, because I am going to take you into this cave deep underground and I am your guide. I am also the only one who knows the way in or out, and since I have the only flashlight and radio, you better stick close to me and make really sure nothing happens to me, 'cause if it does you may not ever get out." After that I did not have any problems with them. Racial prejudice is part of the American landscape, and I work and live in the American landscape, so you cannot escape it.

Environmental Advocacy and the Future

The American culture at large, including many African Americans, knows very little about the role the 9th Calvary played in Yosemite prior to the creation of the National Park Service. Yosemite was created in 1890, and the Park Service was created in 1916, so between those years the U.S. Army protected Yosemite, Sequoia, and Yellowstone National Parks. What was forgotten was that for three of those years, the 9th Calvary protected Yosemite and Sequoia. The 9th Calvary, along with the 10th Calvary and the 24th and 25th regiments, were known through history as the Buffalo Soldier regiments. That history was essentially forgotten here in Yosemite. I tell it to give African Americans a sense of belonging, a sense of ownership. I think that is one thing the history of this park does—it gives African Americans a foothold in a landscape where generally you don't hear much about African Americans. When I adopt that persona of Elizy Boman, it is a way of connecting emotionally with the social history of what it was like being Black in 1903. When I tell this story in first person, it allows African Americans to access the Yosemite experience through the spirit of a Black soldier who was here about 100 years ago, maybe even standing in the same place as I am today.

It is a means of creating a sense of stewardship and an ancestral and cultural connection to a place. The Yosemite experience for many African Americans may seem like an alien one, until you uncover the Buffalo Soldier story. Some of the soldiers who lived and worked in this park back then may have descendants living in Oakland, California, for all we know, and they have no idea that their great-grandfather was here as a Buffalo Soldier, faithfully protecting the wilderness of one of the nation's largest and oldest national parks.

One of the driving forces behind why I am keeping the Buffalo Soldier story alive revolves around the disconnect African Americans have with the environment. I served in the Peace Corps in West Africa as a seventh grade English teacher in Liberia. There I saw all of these different people from different tribes—the Kru, the Bassa, the Maasai, and the Mandingo; all of them have their own kind of unique relationship with the natural world around them. Seeing that in Africa and then going back to Detroit and not seeing that connection to the land among the African Americans made the disconnect become even more obvious. I was able to see where we were as a culture and where we had been, and then come back here to the United States where the environment does not even come up as an issue in the Black community.

So how do you solve a problem that is not even perceived as being one yet? When I run into African Americans who don't even see it as a problem, or don't see that this problem is their problem, it makes it much harder to solve. How can you have tens of thousands of years of incredible visceral connection with the land and then, in a fairly short period of time, over the course of a few hundred years, have a complete disconnect? Now we have lost our complete identity, because in Africa you were not just African, you were from a specific tribe from a specific region, with your own language and words for the sun, the earth, the water, and animals. Most African Americans do not know what tribe or regions they were from, so they have lost their cultural, ethnic, and specific identity and become just African Americans. How can you have such disruption in a culture without having some psychological or spiritual ramifications? There is a price to be paid spiritually from a disconnect with the natural world.

Shelton has been with the National Park Service for 37 years. In his career, he has impacted so many. From his beginnings as a seasonal ranger at Yellowstone to his current position at Yosemite as Community Engagement Specialist in the Office of Education and Outreach, Shelton has educated countless visitors on the history of the African American Buffalo Soldiers and their essential role in establishing the parks. In my mind, Shelton will always be seen as an important individual responsible for expanding the number of people of color in outdoor spaces. His decades of dedication and determination to ensure that all Americans receive the full benefit of their natural heritage is commendable, and I'm truly honored to know him.

—*Dudley Edmondson*

THE JAMES P. BECKWOURTH MOUNTAIN CLUB was named after a famous biracial African American, James Pierson Beckwourth. He was a true legend of the West.

He was born in 1798 in Fredericksburg County, Virginia, to a white plantation owner and one of his African American female slaves. They moved to Missouri when Jim was about 6 years old, because they wanted to stay together, and it was easier at that time to do that there than it was in Virginia. Beckwourth was raised in Missouri. He was taught to read, as were all of his siblings. He was apprenticed to a blacksmith so he would have a trade. Around 23 years of age, he was fortunate enough to meet General William Ashley, who founded the Rocky Mountain Fur Trading Company. Beckwourth joined the company as a hunter, and over his long fascinating life he was, among other things, a frontiersman and an exceptional explorer. In 1850, he discovered a pass over the Sierra Nevada Mountains that would lead pioneers into the Sacramento Valley of California.

He also saved the life of General Zachary Taylor, who later became President of the United States. Beckwourth was also war chief of the Crow Indian nation. He was adopted into the tribe, and he pretty much lived with the Crow for many years. He spoke a multitude of Native American dialects and was fluent in English, Spanish, and French. He was also one of the co-founders of the city of Pueblo, Colorado.

Our organization named itself in honor of Jim Beckwourth because of his contributions to the West and also because he was a real trailblazer and adventurous guy. We like to think that we honor some of that spirit of adventure and his legacy in our organization.

CHERYL ARMSTRONG

**President and CEO, James P. Beckwourth
Mountain Club
Denver, Colorado**

Cheryl in Golden Gate Canyon State Park near Golden, Colorado,
with a youth group at a Beckwourth Mountain Club Picnic

Childhood Experiences and Turning Points in Nature

I was born in Detroit, Michigan. My father's side of the family was one of the original Black families in Michigan. They founded the first Episcopal churches. My childhood was pretty unusual for African Americans at the time. My father was a doctor, and his father was a doctor and medical school professor, and education had gone on and been a tradition in my family for generations and generations. I guess you could say I had a very affluent childhood.

We had a house in Detroit where my father practiced medicine and proudly served inner-city residents. He also had a home in Canada, across the river right on Lake Saint Clair. So I grew up canoeing, swimming, and hunting in the summer. I fished and explored the woods around our home in Canada. My father had a boat, and we got to water-ski and do all of the traditional water sports. We would ice-skate on the lake in the winter.

I grew up being a very athletic girl. I loved sports and the outdoors and being in the woods, immersed in nature. I loved being under the open night sky more than anything—it was good for the soul then, and it is good for the soul now.

What I Do in the Outdoors

I have been involved with the Beckwourth Club since I moved to Denver in 1995. In 1998, we started a formal program called the Beckwourth

View of rugged ridgetops in Rocky Mountain National Park

Outdoor Education Center. Its specific purpose is to take urban youth into the outdoors to go hiking, fishing, camping, backpacking, snowshoeing, whitewater rafting, canoeing, and kayaking. We teach them mapping and compass skills as well as self-arrest training and leadership skills.

The reason we started the Beckwourth Mountain Club (it was formed in 1993) was because of our passion to bring the outdoors to inner city youth and residents. The organization is run by a terrific group of almost 60 volunteers, predominantly by people of color. They act as mentors, chaperones, hike leaders, instructors, and historical reenactors. They mentor not only the young kids in the organization, but also the adults that come to our center that are new to the outdoors.

The membership is open to everyone and is about 65% African American, 25% Latino, and the remaining is mixed race, multi-race, Asian, Anglo, and all combinations thereof. Membership is for families, singles, and seniors. We do outdoor activities every single weekend, from easy day hikes to climbs of Colorado's peaks. We also do upscale trips such as orca watching on the San Juan Islands off the coast of Washington state, and trips to national parks such as Acadia in Maine and Yellowstone in Wyoming. The idea is to make these national parks and wilderness areas available to a broader population.

I also do a great deal of fundraising. That's my job—I am the money beggar! I am the grant writer and public relations person. I travel around the country heading up panel discussions and workshops, doing presentations on our program. I guess you could say I wear about 15 different hats around here.

I spent many years in the legal profession, but eight years ago I was able to break away and do what I truly love and have a passion for. There is no comparison salary-wise between working for a nonprofit organization and being in the legal profession, but I would not do anything else even if you gave me a million dollars. I enjoy running this organization and doing what we do for the community.

Heroes and Mentors

The most important mentor in my life was my father. I guess you could describe him as a Black Ernest Hemingway. He was a big game hunter and trophy fisherman; he was way ahead of his time. We traveled all around the world during my childhood and did outdoor activities as far back as I can remember.

We would travel to Mexico for fishing and traveled to different countries around the world visiting historic places, climbing the pyramids in Mexico—you name it, we did it. My father traveled to Africa quite a bit in the late 1950s as a big game hunter; he would go on safari there. He also wrote and was a civil and women's rights leader and a great speaker too. I had a great mentor in my father.

Minorities in Our Wild Places

I don't think that African Americans and other people of color spend enough time in the outdoors. The reason, I believe, is because they just don't have the opportunities and access to do so. Getting into the outdoors oftentimes requires transportation, and many urban residents do not have reliable transportation. Another factor is that it takes a certain amount of know-how and equipment to do these things. Many of them simply cannot afford it, nor do they have the skill sets to be able to safely do things like camp or backpack. In order to get that knowledge, they need access to a program or organization like the Beckwourth Mountain Club.

Youth and Wilderness

One of the rewarding parts of running the Beckwourth outdoor and youth program here is experiencing firsthand the joy and awe of children who come through our program. This is Denver, and we come very close to the front range of the Rocky Mountains, with its alpine lakes and flower-filled meadows within an hour or so of the city. However, 87% of the children who come through our program, although born and raised in Denver, have never been to the mountains and seen this breathtaking scenery. Most of them have never experienced what it is like to climb along a mountain trail or have never been camping. Oftentimes when they first have this experience of an overnight of camping, or seeing the night sky away from the city, the looks on their faces are truly remarkable.

People of color, whether they are African, Latino, or Native American, have always had a deep connection to the land.

This is a long-term mentoring program that is not just a one-time camp-out or one-week trip; kids can sign up in our program at early as age 8 and remain in our program until they are age 18, and even after that they can come back and work as part-time program assistants and also as youth leaders. A big part of the program is to not only introduce urban youth to the outdoors, but to seek youths who really enjoy the outdoors, key in on those particular kids, and encourage them to pursue careers in natural resources fields. We help young people with career prep, college scholarships, and summer internships with national partners such as the Park Service, the

Cheryl with her dad in Mexico

Environmental Protection Agency, the U.S. Forest Service, the Bureau of Land Management, and others who are interested in diversifying their workforce.

The keyword here is "diversifying." Everybody is now jumping on the bandwagon because they realize that the population demographics in the country are changing, and if we don't impress upon this younger and more diverse generation the importance of protecting our wilderness areas, then we are all going to be in trouble. It's very important to pass on those ethics and foster stewardship with our young people. Plus, it is important to show them, contrary to what most city residents think, that the outdoors and outdoor activities can be enjoyed by everyone, not just by wealthy or middle-class white people.

Best Outdoor Experiences and Favorite Places

My favorite outdoor activity is and always has been horseback riding. I have been riding since I was 5 years old and still love it. Being on the back of a horse on a trail, climbing up into the mountains and wilderness areas of Colorado makes me feel like I am truly at home. Camping out under the stars and seeing the beauty of the constellations with no light pollution from cities puts me in a whole other state of mind. It relaxes me and takes away all the stress that I may have had. Nothing makes me feel the same way; nothing is even comparable.

Some of my more memorable experiences in the outdoors with my father and my family include touring the ruins of the fabulous city Angkor Wat in Cambodia and climbing the pyramids in the ruins of the ancient Mayan city, Chichen Itza, on the Yucatan Peninsula in Mexico. I remember holding a huge python in Algiers, Morocco, and watching a ceremonial snake dance with live cobras. We also rode camels at sunset in the desert there; it was just beautiful. We rode elephants while in Thailand and Cambodia. My father enjoyed life and enjoyed world travel, and he has given me outdoor experiences I will never forget. I feel very fortunate.

Here in the United States, some of my more memorable experiences include seeing the Grand Canyon at sunrise. And seeing a female grizzly with her cubs and, on the same morning, a wolf pack in the Lamar Valley of Yellowstone National Park. In New Mexico I took a night hike at the cliff dwelling of Bandolier National Monument. We saw thousands and thousands of bats emerging from their caves at dusk.

But my favorite place to spend time outdoors is in Colorado's Rocky Mountain National Park. I say that even though I have traveled all over the world and seen some pretty incredible places. I have been in just about every state in this country, which includes visits to several national parks and state parks, but for me nothing can compare with the beauty of Rocky Mountain National Park.

Being a Face of Color in Remote Places

On field trips with youth groups here in Colorado, the children always notice that whenever we go somewhere hiking or camping, people stare at us. White people stare at our groups of African American or Latino youth or adults—it happens with our group every time we go on a field trip, simply because they are not accustomed to seeing people of color in the outdoors. There is also a certain amount of prejudice in some of the rural areas that we go to, which includes unfriendly and rude staring that is probably meant to intimidate us. The kids always ask why people are staring at them, and we tell them it is because they are special. Our program is very disciplined and structured, and we teach the children to conduct themselves in a very respectable manner so their behavior does not warrant the negative attention they may get.

Environmental Advocacy and the Future

Stewardship might be the most important part of our program here in the Beckwourth Mountain Club. I am very proud of the fact that we not only teach our young people about the environment, but we also teach them the importance of protecting, preserving, and managing this country's natural resources. We do that by partnering with national organizations like the National Park Service, the U.S. Forest Service, Colorado State Parks, and other organizations. Every long trip we do with the youth program also incorporates work projects. The kids not only learn that it is fun being in the outdoors, but they also have to learn how to protect the environment—how to restore trails, how to restore and protect natural habitats—and they learn about different ecosystems and how they function.

I do many presentations about the Beckwourth Mountain Club and its efforts to increase diversity in the outdoors. I have traveled to national conferences around the country as a guest speaker for seminars, panels, and workshops. One comment I frequently hear from non-people-of-color never ceases to amuse me—"I didn't know groups like yours existed!" People of color, whether they are Black, Latino, or Native American, have always had a deep connection to the land. It is part of their culture. They lived on the land, and they survived by living off of the land. It has only been in the last 100 years or so that people of color have become urbanized.

Another frequent comment I hear comes from environmental groups. They are surprised about the results of recent surveys. The surveys showed that people of color who reside in urban areas: (1) want their children to be exposed to the outdoors; (2) are very supportive of protecting the environment; and (3) look forward to opportunities to get into the outdoors. Why should this be surprising? Why would urban residents and people of color not want these opportunities for themselves and their children?

I have not been able to reconnect with Cheryl, but her role in the book was that of a strong voice and advocate for getting BIPOC folks outdoors. Unfortunately, the James P. Beckwourth Mountain Club no longer exists; it later changed its name to Beckwourth Outdoors. At the time, it was one of very few organizations in the country that focused on getting people of color outdoors as well as building these traditions within families of color. They offered outdoor educational opportunities and skill-building outings that really helped youth and adults feel confident about being in the outdoors. Other organizations around the country now offer similar opportunities, but Beckwourth was a leader at the time.

—*Dudley Edmondson*

MY PASSION FOR CLIMBING IS CENTERED
on the challenge it brings. The skills I use during climbing can be applied to everyday life. I may sit there, frustrated, a thousand feet above the ground with a particular climb or route and say to myself, "I think you need to go back down a bit and think the whole thing through again." I will sit there hanging from the rope for a while and go over it in my mind, looking at my successes and my failures and go back up to try it again, trying to solve the problems one at a time until I have succeeded.

I have lived in southwest Missouri for about six months now. I work as a district manager for an insurance consulting company. Prior to moving to Missouri, I was a hedge funds stockbroker in southern California.

Childhood Experiences and Turning Points in Nature

I was born in Chicago and spent the first seven years of my life there. My parents then made the best move ever, relocating to sunny southern California. I think had I stayed on the South Side of Chicago, I probably would have ended up getting more involved in traditional sports. I got my start in the outdoors when my parents sent me to a school called the School of Creative and Performing Arts around the sixth grade. If you remember the show *Fame* from the 1980s, it was kind of like that. Basically, you were doing all of these different things, changing up every four weeks. One month we were doing music, the next month we did dance, and then the next month we did theater—and one week we did camping. I thought, "Wow, this is kind of cool." That at least opened up the door for me, letting me know that it was OK to like the outdoors.

ELLIOTT BOSTON III

Experienced Mountaineer
Springfield, Missouri

Elliott near Mount Evans in the Front Range, Idaho Springs, Colorado

The thing that changed my life forever was when I saw the film *K2* back in 1992. After I saw that movie, I said, "Climbing is the sport for me." You know, it was kind of like trying on a pair of shoes. You try on several pairs and then you find that one pair that are like, "Oooh, these are a perfect fit. This feels good!" I was 22 years old at the time. I got a late start in rock climbing, and then from rock climbing I just got into mountaineering. I started with sport climbing, then I moved to traditional climbing, now I do ice climbing, and eventually I will do some aid climbing. It is a sport I love. I will always be a climber. I can do it when I am 70 years old. One of the things that has always attracted me to doing things outside is that it has no age limitations.

Climbing helps me think outside the box and allows me to be able to handle any stressful situation.

What I Do in the Outdoors

I am trying to become the first African American to summit the seven highest peaks on Earth. Each one lies on a different continent. To date, I have successfully done four of them. I have summited the South American peak, Aconcagua, which is the tallest mountain in the western hemisphere, in Argentina, at 22,841 feet. I have climbed the European peak of Mount Elbrus in Russia, at 18,481 feet. On the African continent, I have climbed the highest peak, Mount Kilimanjaro, at 19,339 feet. And finally, the highest Australian peak is Mount Kosciusko, at 7,000 feet, which I have also climbed. To fund my climbs, I solicit sponsors; these have included Volvo, the North Face, and Pepsi. I do a lot of it out of pocket, tapping my own savings as well, but I could not do it all without generous sponsors.

In my training to climb high-altitude mountains, I do a lot of trail running, mountain biking and working out with weights. I do strength training, not the body building stuff. I like to ride my mountain bike for six hours or more along a trail up by St. Louis. This will help me get ready to go for Everest or my climb of Mount Vincent in Antarctica.

The Spirit and Nature

I am truly at peace when I am out there. When I am out climbing, I could have all the stresses in the world and I do not think about any of them. I am thinking about my next move. Climbing helps me think outside the box and allows me to be able to handle any stressful situation. I say to myself, "Hey, I can do this. If I can hang on the side of a mountain in snow and bad weather for days, I can handle the stress of day-to-day life, no problem."

Mountaineering is dangerous and you can die very easily. I have adopted the philosophy that two of my friends, Conrad Anker and Ed Viesturs, use. Their philosophy is, "Reaching the top is optional. Getting back down is mandatory!" As long as you keep that philosophy in mind, you will keep all your fingers, toes, and nose and try it again another day. I think that philosophy has kept me in the game. People who don't follow that philosophy never come down from the mountain and are never heard from again.

Youth and Wilderness

The message I would like to get across to other African Americans and minorities is that when you think about doing anything in the outdoors, approach it with an open mind. Don't look at it as though, you know, Black people don't do this or that. Because, as always, there are many Black pioneers out there leading the way for others to follow. My word of encouragement is just to say, "Get out there and try something new."

Chugach Range in Alaska

Since I have been here in Missouri, I have talked with a couple of school groups about climbing. The thing I love about talking with kids is that they are so excited about the thing I am bringing to them. A lot of these kids have never been outside of the city limits, let alone seen another continent. So when I go and talk to them about pursuing their dreams, I tell them, "With a little focus and determination, you can achieve just about anything you set your mind to." In doing that I have planted a seed for success. I have watered it; it's germinated and started to grow. From then on it is up to teachers and parents to nourish it. I get letters from kids thanking me for coming out to talk to them. They say, "Thank you for sharing your climbing stories and your passion of climbing." I feel good knowing I have given something back to my community. When I first started this, I was trying to focus on minority kids, but I soon realized that all kids need inspiration.

North Cascades National Park, Washington

Best Outdoor Experiences and Favorite Places

My first conquest in my bid for the seven summits will always be vivid in my mind. It was the first time I had left the continental U.S.A., and I was headed to Russia's Mount Elbrus. I had used a guide company to go out and do this particular climb. I had heard a lot of horror stories about going to Russia, and I did not want to have any problems with the govern-

Elliott on the summit of Mount Kilimanjaro

ment and local criminals. I knew I was making a historical climb, though, so that was very exciting. I was the first African American to climb in Russia!

It was very unfortunate that early in my ascent I was stricken with dysentery diarrhea. It came out of the blue. One day I ate something and the next day I had it. I was shut down. It got so bad that I started to limit my food intake because I knew what would happen to it in my stomach and bowels. Needless to say, my physical strength suffered greatly as a result. The only thing that kept me going was my will and determination. I had diarrhea on the mountain all the way up to the summit. The other climbers were maybe 800 to 900 feet behind me, but it was obvious to all that I had intestinal problems. I was humbled by the entire experience. When I finally reached the summit of the mountain, man, I just broke down in tears and cried like a baby. I was drained physically and emotionally—it all just came out. I had not cried like that since my grandmother died the year before. I did not think I was going to make it to the top. I was weakened by the lack of food and the diarrhea. But the last 60 feet to the summit, I got a burst of energy and I just ran to it and collapsed in tears.

The trip to Africa is a long three days on two 747s. I was in Uganda in 2000, then in Tanzania and Kenya to climb Kilimanjaro in 2003. There is always a connection to Africa. Most of the people are very friendly, and many of them speak English. They feel connected to you because they know that a long time ago you, too, had deep ties to that continent and you are part of them. Once you leave the airport and begin to drive, you are overwhelmed with this beautiful, vast, open countryside. The only real drawback to going to Africa is seeing all the poor people. The poverty was sad to see. But in terms of natural resources, it is an extremely rich continent, perhaps the richest soil you will ever see. The rains in Africa are unbelievable, and once the storm passes it is beautiful. The land becomes so green, the trees and shrubs just pop to life afterwards. The green is so vibrant; it just stays in your mind. I look back at pictures I took there, but they pale in comparison to the memories I have of the place. It is one of those places you have to see to believe how beautiful it is.

Being a Face of Color in Remote Places

Have I experienced racial prejudice in the outdoors? I would say it is not so much of people saying or doing things to me, but more of people staring at me when I am doing what I do. People staring with this look of "Oh, I did not know Black people could climb mountains." When I was in South America, in Argentina, people would ask me, "Well, who do you play soccer for?" When I would tell them I was not there to play soccer but to mountain climb, they would be so surprised and start talking excitedly to one another in Spanish about me. Then in Russia, I was an instant celebrity. I swear, people thought I was Michael Jordan or somebody, because they were saying, "Oh my God, can I have my picture taken with you?" Man, I was anything but fresh smelling, because I had been on the mountain for six or seven days and had not showered, but people were still running up to take my picture.

Environmental Advocacy and the Future

One of the more memorable experiences I have had was a sea kayaking trip I did in Prince William Sound in Alaska. You could follow the coast in your kayak. We saw a few ecotourism vessels showing groups of people glaciers, but other than that we had no human contact for 11 days. We saw all kinds of cool wildlife, like moose, bald eagles, salmon runs, and sea otters. We started campfires from scratch, cooked dinner—it was a very memorable journey. The place was absolutely beautiful! Once you have been to a place like Alaska and seen the vastness of the land, you could spend a lifetime exploring it and never see it all. It kind of gives you a flavor for what

America was like before European settlers moved in. Having grown up with the Exxon Valdez oil spill in the news in 1989, I think that left a big impression on me; that is why I knew the environment would be an important issue to me.

I think that to make sure that there are wild places for future generations, you need to educate people about the existence of these places. People need to know what is out there. It is kind of like the sales market: They have to see its benefits and a fear of loss of those benefits, asking, "What do I stand to lose here?" If people realize that once these natural treasures are gone, they are gone, then they can understand the loss. If you can create that type of awareness in people, then they may be more receptive when major issues of environmental concern arise.

Elliott has always been an ambitious young man. He seemed impatient and bored with ordinary life and wanted nothing less than the grandest life experiences he could conjure. His background as a mountain climber—a traditionally white field in the US—was what initially drew me to him, as well as his willingness to encourage others to embrace the outdoors. In 2018, Elliott was sentenced to federal prison for taking part in a real-estate scam, and he has since been released on parole. I firmly believe that we—all of us—are more than our worst moments, and I believe that Elliott's original message in this book, of exploring the outdoors, still holds true.

—Dudley Edmondson

I LIVE AND WORK FOR THE National Park Service here in Denver, Colorado. The Park Service is the agency designated with America's preservation responsibilities, and it deals in the main with America's natural, cultural, and outdoor recreational heritage.

It is important that we connect all Americans to their natural, cultural, and outdoor heritage, not only because it is their birthright, but it is part of what comes with the package of being an American. We think these places are among the best places in the country not only to learn about the Earth, but to learn about your history as an American, to learn about the multiple stories that make up this mosaic we call America.

They are also great places to learn about yourself. National parks are places where you can be quiet and let the soul think. You can do things by yourself, with your family, with your friends, and with people who you just met that will help you better understand, perhaps, your role in your state, in your society, in your nation, and on the planet. So it is really important, for many reasons and in many ways, that people of color and people of lower economic scenarios who have been dis-invited from part of this conversation be included.

Childhood Experiences and Turning Points in Nature

I grew up in Washington, D.C. My mom was from the District, from a long line of D.C. residents. My dad was from southern Virginia and from a middle-class kind of African American upbringing. My mom and dad were both teachers, my grandparents were teachers, everybody we knew seemed to be teachers. That is kind of how I came up.

BILL GWALTNEY

**Assistant Regional Director for Workforce Enhancement, National Park Service
Denver, Colorado**

I was always interested in the West—its landscape, its peoples, its history. I was driven, in part, like so many 8-year-old kids, by my interest in the Native American culture. Like a lot of African Americans, my family has American Indian ancestry, both the Pamonkey people in Virginia and some of the New England tribes on my mom's side.

My grandparents and I spent a lot of time together because we lived in the same city. My grandfather, who was a World War I veteran before becoming a teacher and a principal and who remained a community activist until his dying day, noticed I had a real thing for John Wayne westerns. So after weeks of this, he came to me one day and said, "You know, when you get done with that John Wayne western, I got some vanilla ice cream in the kitchen for you." Of course, that really focused my 8-year-old attention. Over a bowl of Breyer's vanilla ice cream, my grandfather told me what he knew of African Americans as soldiers, as pioneers, and as trappers in the West. I almost immediately lost interest in those John Wayne westerns. The Saturdays I spent with him after that, for years, were spent at the Library of Congress and at the National Archives, trying to find images of African Americans in the West. We did not find a lot of images, but we found enough. This then gave me the sense, both intellectually and emotionally, that if I wanted to do things western and if I wanted to live in the West, there was a historical precedence for it. So that led me to history, and, in many regards, history led me to the Park Service.

My grandparents had purchased a house in the 1930s at a place called Highland Beach, which is historically an African American community near Annapolis, Maryland. What had happened back in the 1890s was that Frederick Douglass and his second wife went to a public beach, which is still a public beach, on the Chesapeake Bay in Annapolis. Mr. Douglass was evidently recognized from newspaper articles and they said, "Oh, Mr. Douglass, you are the minister to Haiti or something, aren't you?" He said, "Yes, I am," and they said, "Well, that is really great, but you can't come here because this is a segregated beach." Here is a man who had spent his whole life fighting first slavery, and then fighting the Confederacy, and then fighting racism, and he had to get back on the train and go back to Washington. Well, two of his sons, who were Civil War veterans, got angry and decided they were going to try to do something for their dad. What they ended up doing was to hire a white lawyer to represent their interests and look for a piece of beachfront property. As it turned out, this piece

A roaring river runs through a steep canyon in Colorado.

of property was just exactly next door to this private beach from which Mr. Douglass had been excluded. So they purchased this land in the name of this white lawyer, and when the deed was transferred, they were the owners, and so they built their dad a house on the bay looking out across the Chesapeake to the Eastern Shore, where Douglass was born a slave in 1818. They thought this would be a great retirement home for Douglass, but, sadly, he passed the winter of 1894 and never lived in the house.

Highland Beach was a real kids' dreamland because of all of the Black families who had known one another for years, some of them for a hundred years. It was almost as if everybody's house was your house and everybody's family was your family, because all the adults looked out to make sure all the kids were OK at the end of the day. With the ocean and many river inlets at your front door, swimming and canoeing and rowing and sailboating and

Bill with his cousins at Highland Beach, Maryland

crab fishing were all part of the everyday summer life.

The six of us grandkids had the run of the place all summer, and the grandparents would come and be there all summer with us. It was like having your own summer camp. It was a great place to become attached to the outdoors. I lived outdoors. I slept in the grass half the summer, or on the back porch—anything to keep from going inside. That was, I think, an important piece of my understanding and appreciating nature.

Another important piece in my connection with nature is that I was part of a Boy Scout troop. It was Troop 333. The scoutmaster was an African American guy named Phil DeWees. Mr. DeWees had been in World War II and had served as first sergeant of Company A of the 369th Infantry, which was the old, famous regiment known as the Harlem Hell Fighters. He had a tremendous sense of the outdoors and a tremendous comfort in the outdoors.

After I sort of progressed through the scouting program, I worked for the Goshen Scout Counsel camps in Goshen, Virginia, for seven years. I went in as a counselor in training and came out as a camp director.

What I Do in the Outdoors

After 26 years of working for the Park Service, I find myself as an Assistant Regional Director in a very singular job, which attempts to find ways to bring people of color into the parks both as visitors and as employees of the National Park Service workforce. In many regards, the faces of America are not reflected in our workforce at present, and have not been in the past. This becomes very important as America's demographics begin to change markedly. We are trying in a small way to do something about that here at the Park Service, through planning and diversity training, as well as minority recruiting and retention, and by forming strategic partnerships with other organizations.

This is America, is it not? Don't I belong anyplace in America that I want to be? Am I not transportable? This is my native land and these natural resources are a part of my heritage and are here for me to enjoy too.

In my career I have done a lot of different jobs for the Park Service. I started in my hometown of Washington, D.C., at the National Mall, where I worked at the Lincoln Memorial. I am proud to say my career in the outdoors spans over 30 years. I have been a park ranger, a law enforcement officer, and a wild land firefighter. I have been involved in Park Service search-and-rescue activities—pretty much the full range of ranger stuff. I was also Chief of Interpretation at Rocky Mountain National Park. I was the first African American to hold a position like that in that park.

I am able to ask questions that may have never been asked before, like "What role as stewards of American wilderness do we envision for people of color?" That is kind of the role I ended up with. I bring these important issues of race and class and participation to many venues within the National Park system.

A former chief ranger of Rocky Mountain National Park and I worked in offices adjoining each other, and we got to be good friends. One day I said, "You know, we are getting more and more Hispanic users in the park and many of them do not speak English. The ones who do, don't come to the visitors center because we have people with badges and hats." Our park ranger uniform evidently was so attractive that the border patrol copied it almost entirely. Plus in many Central American and South American countries and Mexico, law enforcement officers aren't really your friends. I said, "I think we should look at this and see how it impacts other visitors, and how it impacts the resources, and the fact that it is impacting on Hispanic visitors' experiences. I think we could get ahead of this thing.

"How about during the summer when we get a little extra help, let's get a ranger vehicle and put one of your people and one of my interpretive rangers in it who will speak Spanish and go talk to people. Let's try it on Sunday afternoons after church because most of the folks go to church first before they come up to the park. We'll go around and say the same thing to everybody in the picnic area and the campgrounds, 'Hi, how are you? Have you been here before? Do you know national parks are special? Here is why they are special and here is what you can do to keep them special. By the way, we have free stuff for your kids; we love your kids and we know you do too. We hope you have a good time.'" If they didn't speak English, we spoke Spanish. People were like flowers in the spring—they just blossomed. We hoped they felt more a part of the place and hopefully would become more in tune to the fact that this is an organization that cares about their experience and cares about their family, and if they want to investigate a job opportunity within the parks, they are welcome.

Heroes and Mentors

Certainly one of my biggest heroes and mentors was my grandfather, who aided and abetted me in my interest in the outdoors, even when my grandmother and other family members thought it was a waste of time or passing fad. They thought it was not something that was convertible into an actual job. My dad was very concerned that, even if I were to pursue it, it would be physically dangerous. He thought I might find myself in places where African Americans were not welcome and, in fact, might be attacked. My father lived in a time where he remembered at least five friends or acquaintances who were found lynched or were just never found. This affected him very much and affected his perception of my career choices. He told me he would rather I work for the post office. Not that there is anything wrong with working for the post office, but it was not what I wanted to do.

People like my granddad, who said, "You can do whatever you want to do," and like Phil DeWees, who was very focused in saying, "You can have a career in whatever you want to have a career in and you can be the best, but you have to want it and you have to want to work to get there," were my mentors.

Other heroes were people like Jim Beckwourth. Beckwourth, for me, not only represented an African American with a historical presence in the West, but the whole era of the fur trapper, the mountain man, and suggested to me that he had all of these outdoor skills, which had been honed by his association with native people.

The Spirit and Nature

I think I have all the usual reasons for spending time outdoors; I think it is where people belong. All of the real rhythms that exist in the world are all based on nature—night and day, the four seasons, all of that kind of stuff.

I think that as you find yourself in jobs with more and more responsibilities, as you find yourself faced with the normal everyday challenges of life, and you find yourself raising a family, it's good to be quiet. It's good to get some solitude, and it is good to get on a natural rhythm that connects you, I think, if you are open to it, with whatever spirituality that you have. It reminds you of the very, very, very small role you have personally in a much larger space we call the Earth. For all of those reasons and for lots of others, I think one of the healthiest things people can do is to spend time outside.

Bill Gwaltney as a young man rabbit hunting

Minorities in Our Wild Places

It is hard to say without really good data how much time minorities spend out-of-doors. What we have to take into consideration are trips back down to grandma's farm and fishing in the old fishing hole. Going back to Georgia, going back to Tennessee, going back to North Carolina. There is actually an increasing trend for African Americans to return again to the rural South.

So it all depends on how you define out-of-doors. But if you define out-of-doors as these places we have set aside as a nation, the national parks, national forests, and the places we define as Bureau of Land Management areas, I would say the answer is a resounding "no," they don't spend enough time. I say not enough time because their tax money pays for these places too.

There are several reasons why they don't come, but I think the main one might be there is still a residual fear. There were places throughout the country that you dared not go. There were places that were identified as safe, places that were identified as unsafe, and everything else was a gray area. You stuck to places where you had reasonable assurance that you had people who looked like you, people who would understand your interest and your motives, who would provide goods and services for you. You wanted to deal with people who would treat you with some level of human decency.

Best Outdoor Experiences and Favorite Places

I can remember sleeping under a larch tree, and I have never felt so rested when I awoke; the best bed I have ever been in was under that tree. The taste of trout stuffed with wild meat, and stories around hunting camps. Being alone in the wilderness with the sound of your horse's hooves on rocks along a trail echoing all around you. Water so cold it hurts to drink it. Camping out and waking up in a tent that is covered with a foot and a half of snow. There are so many of these life-changing experiences that I remember. These are things that drive so deeply to the core of who you are as a human being, words really don't suffice. I think they all change your life for the better, because they make you a better person, a more prepared person, and a more connected person.

Being a Face of Color in Remote Places

I remember my dad taking my brother and myself down to where he grew up in Virginia. There was a place called Whataburger and they specialized in these huge hamburgers. My brother and I thought that was the coolest thing going, and we'd say, "Dad, stop. Let's go to Whataburger. They're not that expensive." My dad would say, "They are closed," or "No, it looks like they are too busy." There was always a different excuse. We were smart enough to know they were not closed and that they were not too busy. It was the legacy of racism that prevented him from wanting to stop. It was not money or anything like that; it was that he did not want his sons to see him refused service in a place of business.

Sociologists think that those kinds of stories resound in families for several generations. It may not have happened to me, but it happened to my dad or granddad, my mom or grandmom, and I'm going to be thinking about that. So those kinds of things affect whether or not people of color are willing to take that trip to the Grand Canyon or to Yosemite or Big Bend National Parks. Even if they understand the Park Service will do everything it can to make sure their visit is right, they can't control what happens from the time you leave Cleveland to the time you get back home.

In terms of camping, I cannot say that I ever have run into racial prejudice, but I have talked to people who have had visitors pick up and move their campsite because they awoke to find that a Black couple had camped next to them. More commonly, minority visitors tell me they hear, "Wow, we don't get many of you people here," which on the surface does not seem very negative, but I think that if people in the majority culture found themselves in the face of such a statement, they, too, would be very hurt and upset and insulted. And it is insulting, when you really think about it long enough. You say to yourself, "This is America, is it not? Don't I belong anyplace in America that I want to be? Am I not transportable? This is my native land, and these natural resources are a part of my heritage and are here for me to enjoy too."

Bill worked as Assistant Regional Director of Workforce Enhancement for the National Park Service. I think his work was essential in making the park's staff as ethnic and culturally diverse as it is today. He clearly understood the importance of diverse recruiting and retention for NPS. He knew the impact BIPOC employees could potentially have on the parks and those who visit the parks. Bill and I shared the same hope of making the outdoors as diverse as our nation's cities and towns. Bill has since retired from the parks, but he is still very much involved in all things regarding people of color in the outdoors.

—Dudley Edmondson

I AM SELF-EMPLOYED, THE OWNER OF D.A.P. Consulting, Inc., a software consulting company. I am also the current President of the North American Falconers Association (NAFA).

I am fortunate that I am doing exactly what I want to do. I am what I have always wanted to be. I did not want to be a doctor or a lawyer or anything else; I wanted to be a falconer. And the fact that I'm a falconer and a Black man and president of the largest falconry organization on Earth is beyond my wildest dreams or expectations.

All of my activities are geared towards falconry. It is a way of life. It is not a part of who I am, it is definitely what I am. When I croak, I want my tombstone to say, "Darryl A. Perkins, good falconer, good father, good person" in that order. I drive the kind of SUV I drive because of falconry. I live where I do because of falconry and I do the type of work I do because it affords me the time off and the finances so that I can leave Boston each fall and come here to Kansas or go to Minnesota and hunt. Owning my own business was not a planned thing. I worked as a naturalist for the Interior Department at a visitor center in Bedford, Virginia, in the Blue Ridge Parkway all through college, and thought that I would be a conservation officer or wildlife biologist or something like that the rest of my life.

If the sport of falconry were outlawed in this country tomorrow, I am either an outlaw or living in another part of the world. Not practicing falconry is not an option—that is not part of the deal. Some folks think that falconry is merely getting a bird and starving it into submission to a point where it has to kill something to live. That is not falconry. There is no room for starvation in falconry. Most falconers, myself included, try to

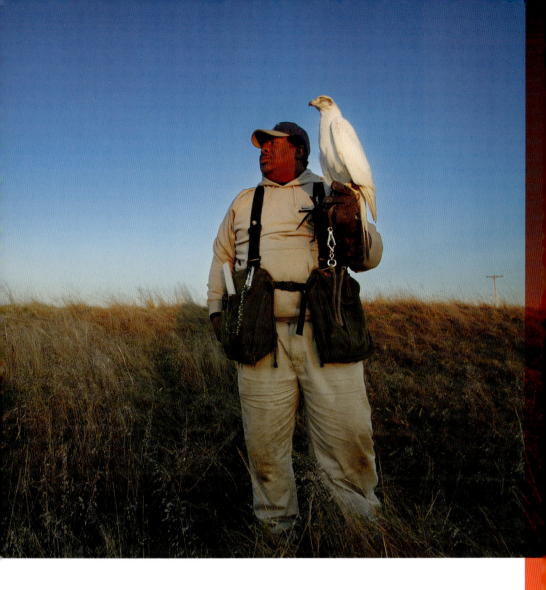

DARRYL PERKINS

Master Falconer
Boston, Massachusetts

Darryl hunting with his Siberian goshawk, Gyrlinka, near Great Bend, Kansas

South Carolina woods

have their birds be as close to what they would be for weight if they were in the wild. Falconry is the art of hunting using trained raptors.

Childhood Experiences and Turning Points in Nature

I was born in 1954 in Lenoir, North Carolina, a small town nestled in the foothills of the Blue Ridge Mountains in the western part of the state. My mother died when I was 13 months old and my father was stricken with polio shortly thereafter, so my grandparents raised me. I had an absolutely wonderful childhood, growing up in a rural community of family and friends. My interest in the outdoors was not a conscious effort. My days as a child were spent exploring the woods, as there was little else to do. As near as I can recall, I have always had an interest in birds of prey. If I saw a buzzard or a hawk, I would watch it.

Growing up in rural North Carolina, in the summer we did not have access to city pools, Little League, or anything like that. The only thing we did have was the bookmobile that used to drive through. It was just like an ice-cream truck; when it came, kids would come pouring out of the woods and out of farmhouses and from everywhere, cheering, and jump on that thing and get a book. You would have to sign the book out, then the bus would come back a week later and you had to turn that one in and get another one. I was always right up front, getting those horse books and dog books and wolf and bear books, because those were the things I was interested in. They used to sweep me off to faraway places, places that I am able to travel to and see as an adult today.

I was introduced to the great outdoors through writers like Jack London and still spend a great deal of my time while in the library in the children's section. That is where all the best books are. The type of books I like to read are full of adventure and excitement. I read *Big Red, Irish Red, Outlaw Red, Lion Hound, Wild Trek,* and *Snow Dog* by Jim Kjelgaard; *The Call of the Wild, White Fang,* and *To Build a Fire* by Jack London; and *The Black Stallio*n series by Walter Farley.

What I Do in the Outdoors

Today, after many years of training as an apprentice falconer and experience in the field, I am in my second term as NAFA president. I am responsible for the day-to-day operation and administration of the organization. Our goals are to promote falconry as a legal field sport, to disseminate information and techniques among interested individuals, and to ensure that the raptorial species we utilize worldwide are conserved and maintained for generations to come.

We have about 4,000 members in the organization worldwide. We represent about 40 different countries, and we come from all walks of life. There is no set occupation or socioeconomic status that defines a person being a falconer. It all stems from a love of raptors.

Heroes and Mentors

My grandfather, whom I consider to be my mentor and who was a pretty good woodsman, told me lots of wilderness adventure stories, which I am sure helped my interest in the outdoors. One of the regrets that I have is that I was not able to share falconry with my grandfather before he died. He died shooting anything with feathers that came across our property. We

Prairie grassland sunrise in southwestern Minnesota

had chickens, so to my grandfather, everything with feathers was a chicken hawk. Made no difference to him whether it was a turkey vulture or what. The thing that got our chickens the most, of course, were Cooper's hawks. My grandfather had a sense of fair play about hunting. We did not shoot sitting rabbits or sitting ducks on the water. We did not shoot quail out of season. But hawks, owls, and weasels, you could shoot on the ground—that was his philosophy. Anytime of the year, and anywhere you saw them. To him, you were doing God's work.

The Spirit and Nature

Nature has always had—I don't know how to express it—a cleansing effect. There is this certain calling, "the call of wild" for lack of better expression, that lures me back to the outdoors and out into nature. No matter whether I am successful at catching something, I still love seeing my hawk fly. The biggest benefit, aside from hunting, is the other things I see and experience when I am out there. When I am out practicing falconry, I might see a box turtle cross the road, or a bald eagle perched in a tree 30 feet away, or a great blue heron with a frog in its beak. Being outdoors places me in a position to enjoy the beauty of nature. It is not a conscious effort on my part to go looking for those things when I am out, they just occur around me and I enjoy watching them. Watching these things connects me to that world, and I record them in my mind and play them over and over again on long nights or long car trips. Nature is one of the things that sustains me.

Best Outdoor Experiences and Favorite Places

Probably the most memorable experience I had in the outdoors was Christmas Day 1989 with my son, Jonathan. He was 18 and had come up from North Carolina to spend Christmas with me on the East Coast. It was about 7 or 8 degrees, windy with light flurries, and generally nasty out. Jonathan and I decided to go duck hunting on Cape Cod. I was living with a friend at the time, and he had a black lab dog named Kala, who I used to take duck hunting with me.

So we went to Cape Cod and went to this place called Black Beach. There are a set of railroad tracks that lead out into a salt marsh. At the edge of the salt marsh there is this really fabulous home. It has a huge deck on the back of it that looks out over the marsh with spotting scopes mounted, so I imagine they watched birds fly into the marsh. I just thought I would take a chance and ask if we could park there. So my son and I went up to the door of this huge house, knocked on the door, and a Caucasian lady answered. I told her I was a falconer and wanted to go hunting on the salt marsh and asked her if I could leave my car parked out there. She said, "Sure, no problem."

I was flying my bird, Lilith, that was a gyrfalcon, prairie and lanner falcon cross, a tri-bred bird. We were walking down the railroad tracks and I had her on my fist, with my son Jonathan and the dog Kala about 10 yards ahead. The railroad tracks were surrounded on both sides by heavy brush and scrub. At the end of this scrub it opened up out into the salt marsh that went on for miles and miles. When Kala got to the edge where the marsh opened up, she froze and stopped dead in her tracks. I told my son, "That means the ducks are in there." It was mid tide, and I peeked around there and I saw this large group of black ducks in this little channel.

For me, for that moment, time just stood still. It was a father, his son, a mongrel dog, and a falcon falling out of the sky.

I stepped back and unhooded the falcon and held her up in the sky, and she took off in typical gyrfalcon fashion. Instead of ringing up, circling up into the sky like a peregrine falcon, she just went up straight away, climbing the whole time like a jet from a runway. She was probably about a half mile away when she turned the first time, still climbing, but now flying back towards my son, the dog, and me. By now she is about 800 feet up, and she comes across the sky over us and the ducks, so now they are pinned down and will not flush because they now know she is up there. Then she heads on her next out run, still climbing higher and higher, and now is about 1,000 feet up. She turns again and this time I lose sight of her. I tell my son, "I lost her, John!" and he says, "Oh, Daddy, I got her, she is just a speck up there! She is right above us." So that was my cue from the falcon to run out into the salt marsh and scream—"Hoo...hooo!"—to flush the ducks. They explode from the water and start flying off. I look up and see Lilith dropping out of the sky. You could hear that sound that falconers say reminds them of bacon sizzling on the griddle. It is made by the wind going through the bells on her legs as she drops from the sky. Like a bolt of lightning from the clouds, she strikes a large male black duck, knocking it onto the ice. John said, "Did you hear that, Daddy?" I said, "Oh, yeah! Sounded like a 100-mile-an-hour fastball popping into a leather glove." Lilith pulled up afterwards like a plane from a nosedive and circled around and headed back towards her downed quarry.

In most cases, the hawk's quarry is killed instantly upon impact, but this duck was not quite dead yet. So she landed on the ice and was struggling with it when they both fell into the open icy water. "We can't get out on this ice, it is too thin. It will never hold us," I told Jonathan. So I decided to send the dog out, so she could drag the duck back on the ice, and the falcon could hang onto the duck. The dog got about halfway there and she broke through. I said, "If it can't hold the dog, it would never hold me."

I was afraid the falcon would freeze up and never be able to get out of the water. Now the temperature had dropped to below zero. The dog made it back to shore with us and I was trying figure out what to do next. I looked at the falcon through the binoculars, and she was all fluffed up, and she was wet and had started to freeze up. I said to John, "Maybe we can go to the other side and I can get her that way." So we got into the car, we drove out and around to the other side of the beach, and I got out of the car and started to make my way through the brush and sea grass, and I, too, fell through the ice. It was up to my waist. I was able to get out, but as soon as I did, my pants froze up. We drove back to the other side and tried to get her to come to the lure I had in my vest. I swung it around and around over my head. She would not come over. She just kept looking down in the trench near her feet, so I figured that duck was probably hiding somewhere down there. I knew she would never come to the lure as long as she thought she could get that duck.

Adult northern goshawk in flight, Duluth, Minnesota

I turned and noticed that there was a lady walking down the railroad tracks. She said, "I have been watching you through my binoculars and figured you needed help. My husband has a dingy rubber raft in the basement, and you can use it to try to get to your bird if you want." So we walked over to her house and went into the basement and got the raft out. The only way I could move it along over the ice was to stand up and scoot along in it, shuffling my feet. When I got over to Lilith, I noticed that she had killed the duck and it was still lying in the water because it was too big for her to pull out on the bank. I got the duck, got Lilith up, and got her into the boat and hooded her. She was hard as a rock; her feathers had all but completely frozen over. Other than that, she would be fine.

So I made it back to shore and the lady said, "You must be frozen. Why don't you come back to the house and warm up?" So John and I went back to her house. She said, "My husband is about your size; you can borrow some of his clothes." Normally when I go duck hunting, I bring extra clothes, but not this time. So while she fixed hot chocolate for my son and me, I took a hot shower and put her husband's clothes on. It is not every day that a white lady on the Cape invites a Black man and his son into her house and lets him take a shower and wear her husband's clothes. Her husband was the local county sheriff. She was a very hospitable lady and I could not have gotten my bird back without her help.

Now the other thing I remembered the most about that day was when John said, "I see her, Daddy!" And the falcon started dropping out of the sky, and the ducks were flushing and exploding from the surface of the marsh. For me, for that moment, time just stood still. It was a father, his son, a mongrel dog, and a falcon falling out of the sky. Now for me, that is what falconry is all about, and what being in the outdoors is all about. It removes all the stresses of daily life.

Darryl is now former president of the North American Falconers Association after serving six terms, but he is still very active in the sport. He is also a well sought-after public speaker and published author. As he is a Black man involved in the sport of falconry, I felt it was important for young Black children to know that what Darryl does for a living is possible. Like so many people in this book, I felt Darryl opened the realm of possibilities for readers, creating a set of outdoor role models for Black folks nationwide.

—*Dudley Edmondson*

THE BIGGEST THING NATURE PROVIDES FOR me is a higher quality of life. I feel connected to nature when I am in it, whether it is an urban green space or a wilderness one.

My preference in wilderness is being away from developed areas, away from modern technology. You will not see me bringing any GPS device. I am a traditionalist and would rather use an old-fashioned compass. To me, that is what the wilderness is all about, getting back to basics—leave the high-tech gadgets at home. I want to be immersed in nature for nature's sake.

Life is full of stress, you know. Every damn day life has always been that way, and probably always will be for many of us. I am middle-aged. I ask myself sometimes, "Was life simpler when I was in my twenties? Was it really truly simpler?" The stresses are only different. But appreciating nature keeps me grounded and sane in some ways. It keeps me focused. I consider myself to be a critical thinker, and if I get stuck or if I am unsure about how to solve something, then I will spend time in nature to help me with the evolution of those thoughts and decisions.

Childhood Experiences and Turning Points in Nature

I grew up as a kid in the 1960s and 1970s, when computer technology was virtually nonexistent—no Game Boys, none of that stuff. My siblings and I, along with my friends, would spend every day outside. I was born in Queens, New York, but I grew up in the suburbs of major cities in the Northeast, outside of Boston, Philadelphia, and D.C. There were always parks, forests, and outdoor spaces everywhere we lived.

Also, being by the ocean, we spent a lot of time on the beach, and for me it was the kind of thing

NINA ROBERTS

Educational Outreach Specialist, National Park Service
Fort Collins, Colorado

where my mother had to drag us in the house for dinner. We were out until dark pretty much every day, and even more so on weekends.

When the school year ended, my parents, like many, sent us to camp. There was something about the camp environment that I truly loved, and there were other parts I absolutely hated. The things I enjoyed, I realized over time, got me thinking about my own career. I became a camp counselor because, at that time, I was ready to get away from home. I worked at this camp in western Massachusetts, which is really where my career in the outdoors started. Spending time with teenage peers, I developed and learned leadership skills while learning about the outdoor activities. I taught everything from canoeing to backpacking and arts and crafts. I did that for three summers before I went away to college, and it was that camp experience that made me know what I wanted to do with my life.

What I Do in the Outdoors

I currently work for the National Park Service as an educational outreach specialist. I work for the entire park system, nationwide. I work with teachers across the country in a variety of ways, as well as park staff and park interpretive staff.

Nina joyfully leaping around on the rocks during our photo shoot

I am also in the process of finishing my Ph.D. in natural resource management in parks and protected areas. My primary emphasis is on the human dimension, working with populations and their understanding and appreciation of the Earth's natural resources from a quality-of-life and recreation standpoint.

I have worked, mostly with high school students, in everything from environmental education to adventure-based programs. And there are fewer and fewer women and girls participating in outdoor activities today than ever before, and there are a lot of myths and stereotypes that exist. So I have also worked with all-girl programs that provide a safe base for young girls to actually enjoy themselves, be free of gender stereotypes, and learn about the benefits of participating in outdoor activities.

Heroes and Mentors

Heroes and mentors are two different things to me. Some of my heroes were people like author Rachel Carson. She was one of the first women to work for the Fish and Wildlife Service. The woman was absolutely amazing in terms of her perseverance and her scholarship. She was a researcher; she was a lover of the outdoors. She spent her time in Maine, on the ocean. Birding was a big thing that she did, but her drive to push the government to realize the dangers of what was occurring with industry is what earned her a place in history. Her legacy was bringing to the spotlight the dangers of DDT from pesticides. She showed how it affected the entire ecosystem, not just the birds, not just the water, but how it is all interrelated—she was one of the foremothers in doing that.

Another of my heroes was my grandfather. He passed in June of 2003. He was from St. Lucia, in the Caribbean; he endured a lot of hardships growing up as a little boy living in the West Indies. He emigrated to the U.S. with his mother, and he was around when everything in this country was separate—Black only, white only. He told me stories of what it was like living in that kind of place. The reason why he is such a hero to me is there are very few people in this world who do not judge other people. He was the kind of guy who truly believed that if you have nothing nice to say, then say nothing at all. He saw the good in everybody.

While you can learn from your heroes, mentors, for me, are individuals in your life who can teach you and they can also learn from you through your experiences. They see your skills and potential. They strive to help make you shine, and will also be honest with you about adverse qualities that you may have that are not going to get you where you want to be.

In this group of folks is a former undergraduate advisor in Massachusetts, a woman named Jan Harris. I have known her for 25 years, and we are still in contact with one another to this day. She helped me get to where I am today. Jim Early is an executive director of an outdoor education center. He gave me my first job out of school as an undergraduate in 1983. He taught me more or less what I needed to know to run an effective outdoor education center. Like all great mentors, none of them tried to stop me from doing what I wanted to do; they just helped me to channel my energies in the right direction to get my objectives accomplished and to affect change in a positive way.

The Spirit and Nature

Nature is very sacred to me. It purifies my thoughts, removing negative energy and stress. I find that, from that perspective, nature takes care of me. I go to nature for those reasons. I feel like when I walk out of it, or when I come off the trail or whatever, I am taken care of. The psychological healing properties of wilderness became clear to me nearly 20 years ago when I was in a near-fatal auto accident. This happened when I was in Boston, right out of college. Not only did that change my life, it changed my way of living, appreciating the things and people around me more. So wilderness gives me an opportunity to thank a higher power for the fact that I am still alive and that my job on this Earth is not yet done. For me, that is a powerful concept, a powerful reality that wilderness has offered me over the course of my adult life. Nature is a very important aspect of who I am. It feeds my soul.

Black people don't see Black faces in the outdoors, so they think it is not for them.

Minorities in Our Wild Places

There is too much disparity in the Black community and other minority communities to believe that economics is the sole factor for lack of participation and spending time in the outdoors. In my research over the last 12 years, I have found that economics is only part of the equation. I am not omitting it at all—the reality is there is still a disparity in terms of wages. But there are lots of wealthy minorities in this country. These Black people are still not spending time in the wilderness. There is a huge growing middle class of affluent Blacks, which means we are comfortable, we have food on the table, we have our own houses, we have cars, our kids are in good schools. The opportunities are there, but life priorities might be different than white people's priorities.

I believe that another part of the equation is very cultural. If you look at the historical background, African Americans could never go to national parks and places like that before the civil rights movement. Today, 40 years post-civil rights, there is no legal exclusion for Black people or any minorities to go anywhere, but history plays a part in people's thinking. Today, kids still believe that the wilderness is an unsafe place to go. For example, here in the Denver area, some of the young people I have interviewed for my research said, "My granddaddy told me the KKK hangs out in those mountains. I ain't goin' up in those mountains!" So again, times have changed, but still that impacts people's decision-making today.

When you combine the country's history on race relations with the stories passed down from generations, then discomfort and safety impact people's decision-making. These factors are a little different for women than men; in general, women have different issues with regards to safety than men, but from a racial and cultural standpoint, discomfort and safety become huge issues in the outdoor experiences of minorities.

Still another factor is lack of knowledge. That is where education comes in—to educate people who have not experienced the wilderness and the outdoors, and to influence those who maybe have gone out but had a bad experience and may want to go try again.

And how do we get outdoor product companies to change their marketing strategies to include minorities? Black people don't see Black faces in the outdoors, so they think it is not for them. Marketing is huge, marketing has a bigger influence sometimes than people realize.

Youth and Wilderness

Many people who live in the inner city take their kids to the local city parks and let them get their feet wet in the water, let them climb on the rocks and up trees. People want their kids to touch, feel, taste, and smell nature. They are in the outdoors, it is public land that is green space. It is important for children in the city to be able to explore nature where they live. To some people, wildlife is squirrels and pigeons. If they learn to respect the animals where they live, they will learn to respect creatures in wilderness areas and begin to understand the full ecosystem better.

For young minorities who are interested in establishing a career for themselves in nature, the more positive mentors they have who are minority people, the better. That is why the recruitment effort for minority instructors is so heavy in outdoor education programs that work with inner-city kids. I had mostly white instructors in the program I was in as a kid, but that was not a big deal to me because my father is white. But for some Black kids it is a big deal. White people are making decisions all

A Colorado hillside of golden grasses in the late-day sun

around them—their teachers are white, the government is white, everybody around them is white—so their minds are saying, "Where are the people in these programs who look like me?" As an adult, when I started working in these outdoor education programs instructing minority youth, it was clear to me that my presence had a huge impact on their learning, because they had a connection with me that they may not have had with a white person.

There is a whole sociological phenomenon in the Black community that says, "Mom and Dad said I need to be a doctor. Mom and Dad said I need to be a lawyer. They never had the opportunity, so they want me to have the opportunity." There is that whole myth of "You don't make enough money in outdoor careers." That is simply not true. At the same time, life is not all about the salary you make. I would never try to turn a young person away from pursuing money by any means, but I would like for them to know that you can make a decent salary in a natural resources career and be very comfortable. Minority kids should learn there is a career opportunity for them if they want to be a wildlife biologist, ornithologist, air-quality specialist, or whatever.

Best Outdoor Experiences and Favorite Places

I had an opportunity to spend some time at the National Outdoor Leadership School, or NOLS. The primary purpose of the course was to continue to help you evolve or develop any outdoor skills you had so that you could be a better leader. There were 12 participants and 4 leaders. A Latino guy and I were the only minorities. We were also the oldest. Most of the other folks were in their early twenties. The program I was in took place in southwest Arizona, just outside Tucson, in a place called the Galiuros Mountain Range.

Everybody had a chance to teach others in the group skills they had an expertise in, so part of the course was to learn from other people.

We spent the month of February in the wilderness, primarily riparian desert environment. That was a new opportunity for me. As much time as I have spent in the outdoors, I had never done anything like that. That is part of why it was so memorable. I've done multi-day trips—10 days, 2 weeks—but I had never done anything like this before. Most of the time the weather was beautiful, lots of sun and nice temps. One night we camped in a saddle in the mountains. There was a change in the weather patterns that night that none of the four guides had anticipated. It started to snow and it was not letting up. The snowfall got heavier and heavier! So the decision was made in the middle of the night, and they woke us up to get prepared to leave the mountains in a rush because we did not have winter gear. This was not a winter camping trip. By the time we were making our way down the mountain, we were walking through 3 to 4 inches of snow with no winter gear. It was whiteout snow, blowing hard, making it nearly impossible to see where we were going. But aside from that, the month-long adventure was great.

Nina was an amazing human being, with such energy and a zest for living. She unfortunately passed away in March of 2022 from pancreatic cancer. It was a very heavy blow to me and so many in the education and outdoor community. She'd become a professor at San Francisco State University in the Department of Recreation, Parks and Tourism. Before she passed, she'd been working on a book project with friends and colleagues entitled *Diversity, Equity, Inclusion & Belonging—Stories of Lived Experiences.* They were able finish it and gave me the honor of having one of my photos on the cover.

Nina was so instrumental in the making of the original edition of this book. She connected me to so many people and really opened my eyes to some of the issues surrounding Black folks and the outdoors. She was way ahead of her time in her vision of understanding the role BIPOC people will play in the future of conservation and outdoor recreation.

—*Dudley Edmondson*

I AM THE ASSISTANT SECRETARY OF the Department of the Interior for the U.S. Fish and Wildlife Department and the National Park Service. The directors of those two bureaus report to me. I am responsible to the Secretary of the Interior for seeing that those bureaus function well. It is up to me to ensure that they function, in terms of budget and policy and personnel, and also that they have what they need to carry out their jobs and functions, from bottom to top.

On a typical day, I spend time with the directors of the Park Service and Fish and Wildlife, as well as spending time up on Capitol Hill testifying before Congress or dealing with the budgets of those two bureaus. Also I may have to meet with congressmen who have issues they want to discuss, wanting a new park unit in their district—and it seems like every congressman wants a new park in their district or wants one expanded or changed in some fashion. Or something may have happened in a park unit in a congressman's district that they may have liked or disliked, and typically they call me when the latter happens. So I talk with them about that and explain to them what we are doing and why we are doing it, or tell them I will have to look into it.

I find that I enjoy the days out of Washington, D.C., when I get to go out to a park unit and see things on the ground and spend time with the people that are doing what I call the "real work." In the four years that I have been Assistant Secretary, I have been to 47 states and visited several of the 384 national park units and many of the 538 national wildlife refuges I oversee. We have 30,000 employees altogether, managing some 178 million acres of land. I have visited with a number of them, but certainly not all 30,000 of

CRAIG MANSON

Assistant Secretary of the Department of the Interior
Washington, D.C.

them. On those trips, in addition to talking with our employees, I will also talk with the general public in and around the parks and refuges and see what their perspective is and get an idea of what they are doing and what we can do to serve them better.

Scenic view along the road to Mammoth Hot Springs in Yellowstone National Park

Childhood Experiences and Turning Points in Nature

As a child, I never imagined that I would have a job like this. I grew up primarily on military bases in New Mexico and California. In New Mexico, the base we lived on had a lot of open space around it. There I learned to really appreciate the desert. A lot of people don't understand the desert habitat. To them the desert is a barren, ugly wasteland. When you live there, you understand it and you realize it is a very beautiful place. So I have quite an attraction to the Southwest and the desert, having spent a lot of time growing up there, involved in scouting, where we camped, fished and hiked in the mountains of New Mexico. The outdoors was a very important part of my life as a kid growing up in New Mexico.

The other part of it for me is that my father is from the Texas Gulf Coast region, and one of the things I remember very vividly growing up is a trip that my grandparents took me on to southern Texas. That was the first time I ever went ocean fishing in the Gulf and saw a very different environment from the desert-and-mountain habitat I was accustomed to. Fishing in mountain streams and fishing in the ocean are very different experiences, but fun nonetheless. Later my family moved from New Mexico to California, and my grandmother, who I don't think ever went past the seventh or eighth grade but was an extremely smart woman, gave me an old book on marine biology as a going-away gift. Turns out, it came in handy, because I had a teacher in California, when I got in high school, who taught us marine biology.

All of that kind of contributed to my background in the outdoors. It grounded me and gave me an appreciation for natural things, although I never imagined I would be in a position such as this where I had something directly to do with the environment from a management or policy perspective.

Heroes and Mentors

In terms of heroes and mentors, for me they have always been teachers, quite frankly. My mother was a teacher in the beginning of her career, and I mentioned my marine biology teacher in high school; these people I've always looked up to and they've shown me pathways in life. So as an adult I have always been interested in teaching. I am very grateful to people who've taken the time to teach me things over the years.

The Spirit and Nature

To me, being in the outdoors and being in wild places has always been a restorative kind of thing. I like people and I enjoy being around them, but I also like being away from the crowds a lot and I enjoy the solitude of places. I was talking about the desert earlier, and there is a certain solitude there that I like. There is a particular quiet in the desert, and I use it as a measuring device and compare other places to it, to determine whether I am happy in a place or not. Once I moved to California, it took some getting used to the ocean environment. There are places on the coast, and this may sound strange, but they are comparable to the desert in terms of their quietness, solitude, and restorative powers, and that is how I know I like them, because they remind me of the desert.

Minorities in Our Wild Places

I have been very concerned about this issue of African Americans and other minorities spending enough time in the wilderness areas, national parks, and wildlife refuges. I have heard some people say, "Oh, that is not for us." I have heard other people say, "Oh, that is something they just don't do." To me, those things are not foregone facts; it is a question of information and access and opportunities. Even I have fallen into these traps, because I have not seen many African Americans and other minorities in these places, and when I fall into those traps I am kind of brought up short. I went down to Grambling University and was at a conference, and there was an African American fellow down there talking about wildlife refuges.

Canyonlands National Park, one of many public lands Craig oversees

He was extremely knowledgeable and I walked up to him and said, "Man, you sure know a lot about wildlife refuges." And he said, "Well, I should. I am the manager of one." I was very embarrassed, as I had never seen a Black wildlife refuge manager and I had naturally assumed that he could not have been one. So I had fallen into the same kind of thinking about what exactly African Americans do or don't do.

So we have got to have exposure, and more access and education for everybody, so that everybody knows that these lands belong to everyone and that everyone is given the opportunity to use them and enjoy them.

. . . when you are enjoying nature, the notion of a shared experience binds people together, more so than any other circumstance . . .

One of the things I am concerned about is the increasing rate of urbanization and the growing concentration of African Americans and other minorities in these areas. That, I think, tends to shut off access, and that is where some of the myths about what people do and don't do build. That is why it is important that we do everything we can to get children in particular into these areas. I have seen many programs around the nation that have had success working on this issue.

I think minority youth definitely benefit from wilderness experiences in a number of ways, from the solitude and quietness experience, as well as educationally. It also opens up economic benefits, letting them know about opportunities for careers in the outdoors. There are so many jobs out there that are available and so few minority youth pursuing them, in terms of natural resource and wildlife management. The jobs are there and we need to expose minority youth to them, letting them know this is a legitimate career path for them. Biology and environmental science are all educational choices that we need to encourage kids to pursue.

Best Outdoor Experiences and Favorite Places

One of my most memorable experiences in the outdoors is one that is both good and bad. A friend of mine is a game warden in Wyoming and for years he has been saying to me, "Let's take this horse pack trip into the Big Horn Mountains," which is an all-wilderness area. The only way in is on horseback, because there are no motorized vehicles allowed in at all. So finally, about three years ago, I went with him and three other guys from the Wyoming Game and Fish Department. We rode horses into the Big Horns, and there were places along the horse trail where it seemed to be only a few inches wide. I would look down the side of that trail off the mountainside, and there would be a drop-off of hundreds of feet. My instinct, because I do not ride horses that often, was to get off the horse and walk. I say that laughing now, but at the time it did not look safe to me and I was concerned. My friend said, "Look, you have to trust the horse, because first of all the horse does not want to fall off the side of the mountain any more than you do, and secondly the horse knows the trail better than you do!" So I said, "OK, I am going to trust the horse."

We made it into the wilderness, to the site where we were going to camp for six days. We set up camp for a couple of days along this creek and we fished a couple of evenings. Then one night, halfway into our trip, it started to rain while we were fishing about half a mile upstream from where we had camped. We started heading back to camp for shelter and I unfortunately stepped on a wet log and lost my footing. So I slipped and fell and thought I had broken my thigh bone—that is how intense the pain was. I could barely walk as a result. After the fellas applied some cowboy anesthetics that they brought along, they decided they had to get me out of there. So the only way out was the same way we came in, and that was on horseback. They could not tell if the bone was broken, but they could not risk it. Needless to say, it is pretty difficult to ride a horse when you have only one good leg—the horse wants to keep going around in circles because it does not understand why you are only using one leg.

We rode several miles before we came upon a Forest Service crew that was cutting some timber in the Big Horn National Forest, and we were at an elevation of about 9,000 feet, so that was another factor. The crew said they had a truck that was just outside the boundaries of the wilderness area and they could take us the rest of the way down from there, but we had to ride on horseback until that point. So we rode another mile back to the Forest Service camp where they had the truck. Just as we got there, the horse I was on tossed me off onto the ground, adding insult to injury. I laugh about it now, but when I got in that truck and we started down the road, I felt every bump, stump, and rock in it going down that mountain. It was a fun trip up until that point. Even looking back on it, it was still an incredible adventure. I keep telling my wife that it was a good trip, even though she disagrees. Any trip you catch fish on is a good trip! It is just one of those things that can happen in the wilderness and that you have to deal with.

Being a Face of Color in Remote Places

Issues of racial prejudice in the outdoors are important because I think it is a key concern that African Americans have. I do think that it is one of the myths, frankly, because it is far often the exception rather than the rule in the wilderness and on our public lands. On the trip into the Big Horn Wilderness Area on horseback, race was not an issue for any of the people I was with, none of whom were minorities except for me. None of the people we came in contact with on our way in or out of the wilderness area were minority, nor did any of them have concerns about race. The majority of the people you come in contact with in those settings are mostly interested in the shared experience. In fact, when you are enjoying nature, the notion of a shared experience binds people together, more so than any other circumstance, and that has been my experience.

In terms of using the resources, there are all the restorative mental benefits that exist and the additional psychological benefit of an almost prejudice-free experience as well. Fear of racism simply should not be a reason to not use and enjoy the natural resources. They belong to you and you should exercise your right to them. You should enjoy them, because you are paying for them with your tax dollars. It is as much a part of your legacy and natural treasure as anybody else's.

Environmental Advocacy and the Future

Ultimately, issues of cleaning up the environment are the same for all people, regardless of ethnicity. There are concerns about environmental justice, in terms of minority communities in close proximity to hazardous waste, but that is an issue for everyone to be concerned about. It is an issue, though, that brings home the point even more of why we need to sensitize minority youth to issues that involve biology and environmental science, so they can understand and recognize things that impact their particular communities. Then we need to help them take those issues to the larger communities as well, which, in turn, helps the larger communities recognize issues in minority communities.

At the time of this book's original publication in 2006, Craig was the highest-ranking Black American in conservation, which made him a must-have interview. His work and place in history are even more important today as more and more Black Americans and other people of color explore outdoor spaces and are appointed to high-ranking positions in government and nonprofit conservation organizations. Meeting Craig was a true honor for me, as I did not know him previously. The original book's major funder, Watchable Wildlife President Jim Mallman, made sure I got that interview, and I am forever grateful to him now.

—Dudley Edmondson

I AM RETIRED—YAY! I RETIRED FROM teaching after 45 years as a modern dance instructor. I taught first at the University of Massachusetts in Amherst. Then in 1971, I came to Detroit to teach at Wayne State University until I retired. I really did not get into birding until I came to Detroit. The campus in Massachusetts was residential, so all of the faculty and students were there. Everybody knew each other and it was a very cozy, nice little setup. When I came to Michigan, I found that it was a commuter campus, so people came in, taught their classes, and went home. I began to feel as though I did not really know anyone at all.

I saw an advertisement for classes through the university center for adult education. The first course I took was "Woody Plants of Michigan." It was fun, but I don't think I really met any new people or made any new friends there. Again, people sort of came to class and then they went home. The next term I took "Birds." That was in the mid-1970s, and from then on I was hooked! The course instructor recommended that we join the National Audubon Society. So I joined and have been a bird-watcher ever since, some 30 years now. It was great—besides the beautiful birds, I met very nice people. I also got to know the area well enough to feel as though I was back home in Massachusetts. With birding, you get to know the areas around where you live pretty well.

Childhood Experiences and Turning Points in Nature

I was born in New York City in 1933 and lived there until I was 5 years old. From there, I went to live on a farm in southern Indiana with my grandparents. I knew absolutely nothing about the out-of-doors then. For a city kid to be

GEORGIA REID

Bird-watcher
Detroit, Michigan

deposited on a farm so young was one of the most wonderful things that could have ever happened to me. I lived on the farm for five years and then I moved back to New York. Moved into a town about 25 miles outside New York City, in a suburban area called White Plains, until I graduated from high school.

It was in White Plains that I got my introduction to the Girl Scouts. I think it sort of allowed me to maintain my contact with the out-of-doors activities that I had learned from living on the farm. The original troop I was in was all African American girls. I went camping in the Girl Scouts when everybody else in my neighborhood thought it was a dumb thing to do. I was one of the Scouts responsible for setting up the campsite for the World Encampment. This must have been in 1948 or 1949. It was held in Cooperstown, New York. There were groups from all over the country that were trained to set up campsites. I remained a Girl Scout through high school. I was the only one in my group who stayed with it that long.

What I Do in the Outdoors

I spend as much time as I can trying to become a better birder. I would go birding on the weekends by myself when I was teaching and be so excited about what I had seen that I would walk into class the following Monday and say to my class, "Guess what I saw this weekend?" The kids were very polite and they would let me go through my little story, trying not to be rude to me. About two years after I started birding, I finally got over the newness of it and I did not feel the need to subject my poor students to birding stories. Then one day a student walked up to me and said, "Don't you go birding anymore?" I said, "Yes, I do. Why?" She said, "My friend told me to take your class because there was this crazy lady who put on this show every Monday morning about the birds she saw over the weekend." So I found out that my students knew me as "the lady who goes birding." It was really nice, actually, because it allowed them to open up and talk about what they had done over the weekend too. They would say, "I was up north this weekend, and I saw an osprey, and I thought about you." It really made them notice things around them more and pay attention to birds.

During migration in the fall, I go birding every weekend. I drive up to Holiday Beach in southwestern Ontario, Canada, at the mouth of the Detroit River. The bird of prey migration there is incredible.

White ibis feeding along a coastal beach

Heroes and Mentors

I can't say I really have any mentors or heroes. I have discovered that I am very much my own person. I don't have to do what everybody else is doing. It does not bother me that if I don't do this or that, that I will be left out—too bad for me, I guess.

When I think of people who have been influential in my life, I would say anybody who introduced me to a new experience. I think that my interest in dance is underpinned by being introduced to theater. When I was a little girl in New York, my mother took me to see the play *Life with Father*. I was 12 years old. It was a very popular Broadway play at the time, back in the mid-to-late 1940s. It had some great actors in it—William Powell, Irene Dunn, and Elizabeth Taylor. My godmother was a jazz fan, and she took me to see all the big bands. I saw Duke Ellington, Count Basie, and whoever was playing the Apollo in Harlem or the Roxy or Radio City Music Hall every week. People like that exposed me to things I would have missed out on had I not known them, and they are important and influential to me.

Sometimes people influence you and don't know it at the time. What you experience or what you learn from them finds its way into your life later. I am a firm believer in trying to provide as many experiences as you can for young people. Even though they may not take to something when it is first put before them, it may become something that they can draw on later in life if they need to.

A sense of adventure about life is a good thing— someone has to be a pioneer and try new things. If you dig deep enough, you will find that African Americans have been everywhere in this country.

The Spirit and Nature

I think it is nice sometimes when you can get into the outdoors and experience the solitude of quiet spaces. You can get a sense of where you are in the universe, especially if you go someplace where there are mountains. You realize how small you are. I think that the place that I felt that feeling the most was in Alaska. The land just goes on forever, you can see so far and wide. You look out and you realize that those glaciers are many miles away and little bitty me is way over here. It really puts life in perspective.

I do not consider myself a religious person. In the out-of-doors, one is introduced to a sense of wonder. It is awesome. That is enough for me. In Alaska, at Point Barrow, I looked down at the tundra under my feet and discovered I was standing in a flowerbed, and the blossoms were all about the size of my little fingernail. I thought to myself, "That is incredible." That is the sense of wonder.

Minorities in Our Wild Places

I don't think that people who live in the city get as much time as they need out-of-doors. Some people seem to think of a vacation as going to Chicago, or Disney World, or something. That is probably because they have never been on a nature trail.

Spending their vacations in out-of-doors places has not been something of interest to African Americans as a group. Several years ago, I was on a birding trip to a place called Indiana Dunes National Lakeshore, and I had a conversation on this topic with the trip leader, who happened to be African American. He reminded me that if you were a Black Southerner, you would not expect to find lodging in the area of the dunes because it would be highly prized by wealthy whites. In fact, you would expect to be discriminated against, and you might feel the best thing to do would be to go back south to the company of other African Americans. So you go back and you visit the family and relatives, and that is a fun and pleasant thing to do. And let's face it, if you are going on vacation you want it to be fun, you want it to be a positive experience. And I think that the very thought that you might have a bad, traumatizing experience keeps a lot of Black people from being adventurous. On the other hand, if you are adventurous, you might find out some things that you did not know before.

I always told my students at Wayne State to get piggy banks and save up all your loose change and you will get enough money to travel across the country. I told them, "You live in an absolutely beautiful country that is worth seeing. New York does not look like Alaska; New York has its beauty, as does Alaska. Give yourself the opportunity to see and experience as much of it as you can."

Best Outdoor Experiences and Favorite Places

I say to everybody, "Go to Alaska!" That, for me, was the trip of a lifetime. It was more spectacular each day. The tour guide would say, "Watch for this bird," and I would be gazing off at the expansive scenery around me.

American robin feeding on mountain ash berries

I take many of my long-distance bird trips with a group from the local nature center. One year we went birding in Alabama, and I remember one afternoon we had a migration movement of tanagers—both scarlet and summer tanagers. It was neat to look up in the trees and see what looked like bright-red Christmas tree ornaments flittering around in the branches. I have also birded the Rio Grande Valley of Texas and seen great kiskadees there. I was birding in Alamos, Mexico, and got to see a toucan—you know, the bird from the Fruit

Loops cereal commercials. There it was in a tree on the side of the road, where we got great looks at it.

Being a Face of Color in Remote Places

Northern Michigan was lumbering country back in the late 1800s and early 1900s. One of the places I have camped on a birding trip was Sleeping Bear National Lakeshore. In the evening, the interpretive staff at the campground put on a visitor program about the history of the area. The program one evening was about logging, and one of the photographs showed a schoolhouse built for the children of the logging workers. There among all the children standing in front of this one-room schoolhouse is one Black child. So there you have a Black person who was adventurous enough to move away from what was available for employment downstate in Michigan, and move his family way up north to be part of lumbering, to make a better life, despite the fact that few Blacks probably lived that far north at the time. A sense of adventure about life is a good thing—someone has to be a pioneer and try new things. If you dig deep enough, you will find that African Americans have been everywhere in this country. It is important to know we have a rich, important history in every state in the Union; you just have to be persistent and seek it out.

You should not be afraid to go where you want. I am not afraid to go wherever I choose in this world. As I say, I started out in Girl Scouts, and that was very supportive and fun, so when I went from my neighborhood Scout groups to my national Scout groups, I met a lot of people who were interested in the things I was interested in and never made an issue of color.

I know that prejudice still exists in this country, but heck, you can find that right here at home. I would say the most unpleasant traumatic experience I ever had with regards to racism was just down the street from here in a city park. If this kid had not been on a bicycle and I had not been a responsible adult, I would have socked him. I was birding along a paved trail and he would ride up to me and say "nigger" and then ride ahead of me, very careful to stay just out of my reach. You know, if I were to allow some poorly raised child to ruin my sense of adventure about the world around me, then he and people who think like him have won.

So don't let the fear that something like that might happen to you keep you from enjoying other places in the out-of-doors. It is beautiful out there and awe-inspiring. Usually the people you meet out there are having the same kind of wonderful experience you are, feeling the same positive emotions you are, and they communicate with you along those lines.

Environmental Advocacy and the Future

I think the agenda for cleaning up the environment in urban areas is divided more along the lines of economics than race. I think that if you are poor and work for a living in a low-paying job, and someone says they are going to build a factory on a site, you say, "Hey, I am a factory worker. I need a job." That person is not so concerned about pollution and the soil contamination that it might cause; they just need to feed their family.

I think that an appreciation of green space comes with having the economic luxury and ability to be able to appreciate it. When you talk about environmental cleanup in urban areas, I think that people there are interested, but a lot of them don't have the knowledge to know how to make their voices heard. Of course, people don't want a waste dump next to their houses, but they don't know where to go to pull the strings to keep that from happening. African Americans have the same agenda as everyone else in this country about a clean environment. They want the same things as everyone else. No one wants to live in an ugly, unhealthy community; it does not matter what color you are.

Georgia passed away in 2012. At the time we met back in the early 2000s, she was one of only two other Black bird-watchers besides myself that I knew. Today, I am pleased to say there are so many more of us. Georgia was such a sweet woman. Our time together all those years ago was very special to me. She was from my parents' generation, so she felt like family to me. She talked about many of the things I knew from conversations with my father. That generation, the "Green Book" Generation, had real safety concerns about traveling throughout the United States as Black folks. Sadly, new generations of Blacks and other people of color find ourselves again burdened with these concerns as the current administration reignites the legacy of America's original sin.

—Dudley Edmondson

ONCE HERE IN COLORADO I WAS working a fire and I helped save a deputy sheriff's life. I was sitting in my firefighting truck on a ridgetop, looking out over the land, listening to the O.J. trial on the radio on a break. All of a sudden I hear these huge water tanker planes flying over, dropping these slurry solutions used to fight fires. So I called in on the radio and asked if they wanted me to go in and help, and they said go in and give them a hand.

The first thing we do in these situations is secure buildings. We make sure people are out and we pull down blinds and shut down electrical power. So I got together a crew of about five people and we were doing that. I tried to call in and tell them how the fire was getting out of hand on us, blowing up all over the place, but I could not get in touch with the commander. I was having radio problems.

Then I told my crew to stay there in the safety zone (you always have to establish one in a fire). So I jump in the deputy sheriff's vehicle with him to try to get to the commander and get us some help on the fire, but the fire cut us off. So I told him we would have to head down the road to a swamp area and seek refuge. The wind was picking up pretty good, sweeping the fire our way. So we got back in the car and started back down the road. The deputy took the wrong road and drove us right into the middle of the fire. I saw the fire sweep across the road behind us and we were cut off.

The timber was pretty tall, 25 to 30 feet. The fire was what we call a top fire, where it travels along through the tree canopy, kind of like the wave people do in a football stadium. Then it drops down in spot fires from that, setting the

ROBERT FOXX

**Former U.S. Forest Service Wild Lands Firefighter
Fort Collins, Colorado**

forest floor ablaze. Fire is an amazing thing to watch. You would swear it was a living, thinking beast. Watching it move, sweeping and swirling, engulfing everything in its path will put the fear of God in you.

Robert meets Al Gore

So the deputy asked me, "What do we do now?" I said, "Get the hell out of here!" So I started down the road running. I looked back, expecting the deputy to be close behind or next to me, but instead he was barely making it. So I went back, grabbed him up, putting his arm around my shoulder. So I am running, nearly dragging this guy down the road. We somehow manage to get out of there and head back to the top of the ridge. We get back up there and the deputy starts telling the crew, "Hey, this guy saved my life. He saved my life!"

We got back to the car after putting out the fire. The steering wheel was all bent up like the Incredible Hulk had gotten to it. The tires had popped and were flat. They said the interior must have gotten up to 800 degrees. If we had been inside, we would have died for sure. All the rubber in the car melted. The fire swept over the vehicle and cooked it!

After I was credited with saving that deputy's life, my crew got to meet Al and Tipper Gore. I sat with a group of nine other firefighters and talked with Tipper, and then I got to meet Al Gore and shake his hand. In the photos I have of us, I am showing Al photos we took of what was left of the deputy sheriff's vehicle after the fire swept over it. He was pretty intrigued with those photos.

Childhood Experiences and Turning Points in Nature

I have been an outdoor person all of my life. I was born in Washington, D.C., but grew up in New Jersey. I grew up as part of a big family. I spent a little of my childhood in the inner city, but most of it was in suburbia. My grandparents had about five acres of land in southern Maryland and they had horses and ponies, so we used to go riding all the time, and stuff like that.

My parents got me into nature by sending me to summer camp right on the Chesapeake Bay. I was encouraged to go, not forced. We used to take the boat that was there and go out on the bay, sailing, about 20 kids or so. We would just get out there and sail around this point of land and just go camp. Or we would take the little sunfish sailboats out, tip them and jump in the water and try to tip them back up again. We would go canoeing and hiking and just try to get ourselves lost and try to find our way back to camp again—just a bunch of kids in the woods having fun and exploring nature. Those were some of the memorable experiences I had as a kid outdoors.

What I Do in the Outdoors

While I was in college at Oregon State University, I worked as a wild land firefighter for the U.S. Forest Service. I ended that career here in Colorado as an engine foreman with a crew of two. My area to work was the Poudre Canyon just outside of Fort Collins. It was my job to patrol that area, keeping an eye out for wild land fires. It was my job to keep my small crew and that truck ready to go into a fire 24 hours a day, 7 days a week at a moment's notice, if necessary.

My Forest Service career began in the town of Oakridge, Oregon. A buddy of mine told me about it. He told me all the money he was making: $15,000 for a summer, not including overtime. So I thought, "Wow, that is a chunk of change. I am going to jump all over that!" The first year, I fought forest fires over summer break from college. In my second year, I stayed with the Forest Service until January, taking a break

Robert Foxx as a wildlands firefighter

from school. Then the following year, I progressed into the "hotshot crew" in Klamath Falls, Oregon.

I've fought lots of fires of all sizes, from 2- or 3-acre fires to 100,000 acres in Idaho. Most of the time you had to hike into the fires with a 30- to 40-pound pack on your back. I used to be the lead sorter, so I used to cut down trees and buck them up or break them down and get all the fire out of them. That was a lot of fun. I learned on the job. Up until that time I had never taken a chain saw and cut down a tree in my life, not before I started fighting fires.

I believe the Earth is our house. You keep it clean and take care of it, and it will take care of you.

I really enjoyed my job. I felt like I was part of a team working for a good cause. I was saving the forest and animals from fire. I also enjoyed all the traveling. Sometimes I would be at a fire for 21 days straight. Then you would go rest up in a nice hotel before going to another fire, sometimes in another state. I remember one time we had just come back from fighting a fire in northern California, and we got back, and on the same day we got another call to go to Idaho and fight another fire. You pack up, get in the plane, and off you go. I enjoyed being flown around in helicopters and getting dropped off on fires and working to put them out. It was very exciting. We worked hard and we played hard. We would hit the bars after we left a fire sometimes. Oftentimes the towns were small, about 5,000 or so people, so the firefighters would pretty much take over the town.

You learn a lot about people and about yourself fighting fires. You work with all kinds of people with different levels of experience, from college kids to seasoned smoke jumpers. You work with people of all races—whites, Native Americans, all with different levels of education. It is a real learning experience. The thing you will find that you all have in common is that you smell like smoke all the time and you are always dirty. You get used to it.

Fatigue sets in all the time. Your muscles get tired and you get blisters on your feet from the heat cooking them in your boots. You say to yourself, "Man, I am not sure how much longer I can do this. " Dehydration sets in, with all the sweating from the heat. Once, in Alaska, I worked 52 hours straight. So it is really kind of a mind-over-matter thing, when you work that long under those kinds of conditions. Everyone needs those kinds of challenges in life. Everybody needs those kinds of things where they can say to themselves, "I can quit here because this is hard, or I can tough it out and be something." It is a real character builder.

Heroes and Mentors

My parents, I would say without a doubt, are my heroes in life. I don't really look to others for that kind of thing. I feel the same way about my own kids—I try to be that kind of person for them. Being a good father to them is extremely important to me. To me, a hero or mentor should be someone I can feel and touch and talk to instead of just a face you see on TV.

The Spirit and Nature

I feel that God created the Earth and nature—they are one and the same. That is part of my reason for being concerned about the environment. God gave us the ability to make our homes and cities, but he also gave us nature and the animals. So I think we need to make sure we take care of the

Poudre River in Poudre Canyon northern front range in Colorado

environment. It is like a house. I believe the Earth is our house. You keep it clean and take care of it, and it will take care of you.

Minorities in Our Wild Places

I think more Black people and minorities need to spend more time in nature. It is something that should be started early in life. Parents need to encourage their children to go outdoors, to go on hiking trips, to go camping and stuff. I was fortunate my parents did that for me. Think about it: If you get a kid interested in nature, then they want to travel and explore the world more. In doing so, they get to meet people from other parts of the world, get to experience other cultures. Even here in the U.S., if you travel to a small community somewhere out in a rural area near a national forest, you will see a very different lifestyle than in the big city.

I think there is a shift in people of color moving from the inner city to suburbia anyway. As more Blacks from the city move to the suburbs and wooded areas, they are introduced to a lot of environmental things. What is suburbia but open spaces? You are getting closer and closer to the environment when you move away from the city. I think, once that shift takes place, you will see even more minorities moving even farther out and exploring the spaces outside the city limits, and they will become more and more environmentally conscious.

Best Outdoor Experiences and Favorite Places

One of the most amazing experiences I ever had in the outdoors was a mountain biking adventure in Moab, Utah. One of the most beautiful areas I have ever seen. Natural arches of red rock everywhere.

When I was there, I did the 12-mile Slickrock Mountain bike trail. It took me all day to do it. I started at like 7 a.m. and did not get done until 7 p.m. It is wild! You're coming down over boulders and stuff 20 feet high, coming down on your back tire. It is scary, but it is a natural rush and lots of fun. You're riding your bike along a canyon rim, and you look over the edge, and it is a 50-foot drop into the canyon below. You know if you go over the side, it's all over baby, and send in the Life Flight choppers!

It was tough, I ain't gonna lie to you; you have to be in good shape. We were there in May, it was like 100 degrees by midmorning or so. But I cannot describe just how beautiful a place it is. There are so many incredible natural rock structures and limestone canyons. It is like God's heaven on Earth there.

Environmental Advocacy and the Future

I think people are not really coming to the realization that global warming is actually taking place. I think it is in full swing. Because our climate is warming up, the land is drying out in many places. Being an experienced forest firefighter, it seems to me that the forest acreage in fires is going up tremendously. A few decades ago you did not hear that much about large forest fires. But now, not only do forest fires seem to be on the increase, but the acreage is enormous—100,000 acres, 200,000. To me, that means there is some tender, dry stuff out there, and that is because of lack of moisture.

I think everyone around the world should be concerned about these global changes. If everybody took a step towards making changes and doing their part to reduce greenhouse gases, it would go a long way in helping solve the problem. Just downsizing your vehicle, getting away from SUVs. Making sure your home is more environmentally friendly and that you are not wasting energy in places, or even looking into wind or solar power as alternatives to natural gas.

When you think about it, we are all on this Earth together, you know. Whether it is the bugs on the ground or the birds in the sky, we are all sort of co-dependent on one another. We are all sharing the same world, so we all need to take care of it.

Robert still lives in Colorado but now in the Denver area. He was someone who I thought of as uncommon at the time as a wildlands firefighter. That type of work is commendable and takes a lot of courage. That career is even more important today as climate change impacts more people and communities across the country.

—*Dudley Edmondson*

I THINK THE REASON I ENJOY spending time in the outdoors is because it rejuvenates and recharges me. I think it is a healthy thing for people to do, especially in this day and age. If my life is any indication for the rest of the population, I find myself just busy, busy—overbooking myself, filling every minute of my time with something. In major cities across the country, people's lives are inundated with billboards, advertisements, TV and radio ads trying to get your attention. It is overstimulation—too much, at least for my mind. As often as possible, I have to get out into nature and get away from all of that overstimulation. Get to a place where it is quiet and you can breathe a sigh of relief. In these spaces, you can hear yourself think again, you can hear the wind and the birds. I would like to help more people be able to see the value in that.

Childhood Experiences and Turning Points in Nature

I had a pretty suburban setting childhood on the outskirts of Chicago and San Diego. In Chicago, if I recall correctly, we were the only Black family in my neighborhood school. I thought it was interesting because no one made a big deal out if it. I think part of that was we were not seen as that threatening. Once our family moved to San Diego, things got a bit more complicated. My new school was more culturally diverse, so there were Hispanic kids, Filipino kids, and more Black kids. These kids told me, "You have to choose which ethnic group you are going to be a part of." I really thought that was wrong. I have always enjoyed the freedom of feeling like I did not belong to any particular race of people, and that people are, after all, just people. I can hang with anybody.

CHELSEA GRIFFIE

Rock Climber
San Francisco, California

Chelsea in California's Marin County on a hillside above
San Francisco Bay, within view of Alcatraz **95**

I don't think there was really any defining moment for me that stands out as the beginning of my enjoying the outdoors. I just remember wanting to camp and be in the mountains. At the time, we were living in suburban Chicago and my parents' response was "Honey, we don't do that." I went camping once with friends in a van at a KOA campground and thought it was nice, but I knew that was not the real camping experience I was after. Camping for me is not centered around technology, electricity, and vehicles. Campground with a "K" is just wrong. I laugh when I say that, but really I don't mean to offend anyone, I just feel that for me it needs to be a little more rustic than that.

The first time I actually did any real outdoor camping stuff was on my own while I was in college. This was before I started climbing. I wanted to do a motorcycle trip and, at the time, I was living in the Bay Area. I asked all my friends if they wanted to go, including my motorcyclist boyfriend at the time, but no one could get away, so I went on my own. The first night I camped by myself in a campground on Moreau Bay. All of the camping stuff was new to me, including how to put up a tent and light a camp stove. But you know what? I figured it out. I did not bring a sleeping pad to go under my sleeping bag because I thought, "Those are for wimps." I discovered that the ground is really, really hard—won't make that mistake again! I learned a lot on that outing about being in the outdoors. I did another motorcycle trip by myself, camping eight days this time. I went along the California coast, over to the east side of the Sierra Nevada Mountains, up through Oregon and back down the coast again.

Sometimes I might be climbing or doing yoga and I am at my edge of my physical abilities, so I am sweating and I am uncomfortable, but in that friction, that is where I learn, and that is where I grow, and that is where I feel the most alive.

What I Do in the Outdoors

I love rock climbing! Rock climbing rocks! I guess I am addicted to it. I have been doing it for nearly 13 years. I danced for several years during and after college. I also practiced several forms of martial arts around the same time, but once I tried rock climbing, it just fit. I like to keep my body fine-tuned and prepared for whatever challenge I put it up to; that is very important to me. I enjoy rock climbing for its problem-solving puzzles, making me figure things out on my own. There is also the physical element. Best of all, I get to be outside and hang out with really cool people in incredible places that are hard to get to any other way. Pulling all of those elements together, it becomes something that I just can't live without. I jones for it!

High Country of Yosemite National Park just before sunset

Even if I am just bouldering, the only thing that is important to me is the 2 square feet of rock in front of my face; it really focuses you. You have to figure out a solution to get up that rock, so your mind is just so focused right there in the moment. It is such a welcome break for your brain, that total focus without the day-to-day distractions. I also enjoy trail running and yoga, but those activities are not as mentally engaging for me as climbing. My

Chelsea practicing yoga in El Capitan Meadow, Yosemite National Park

life can be very hectic—my week's activities are constantly changing—so climbing gives my brain a break to focus on just one thing and shut out the stress of daily life.

Edges are a great metaphor for a lot of things in life. Climbing is all about edges. Yoga is about your edge and working near your edges, pushing yourself into places where you are not quite comfortable, which I think is actually good for you. We all need to challenge ourselves and our thoughts about ourselves from time to time, and be prepared for whatever you must go through to grow as a person. Sometimes I might be climbing or doing yoga and I am at my edge of my physical abilities, so I am sweating and I am uncomfortable, but in that friction, that is where I learn, and that is where I grow, and that is where I feel the most alive.

Heroes and Mentors

My mother is a big hero of mine, although I didn't realize it so much when I was growing up. She is pretty amazing. When I was a kid, she was a nurse, and while she was raising us she put herself through college and then went to Northwestern University and got her MBA. She is just a smart cookie, and very focused, and knew what she wanted from life. She taught us that life was an open book and we could be whatever we wanted to be. There were things that I did not notice my mother doing for me and teaching me as a kid, but now when I see her doing those same things for my nephews, I say, "Now I see. That was orchestrated!"

Other than that, I sort of have mythical heroes, because I did not have any Black female heroes who were amazing athletes when I was a kid. At some point in my life I developed an attraction to being a warrior figure, although I have always felt as though I was born in the wrong time and in the wrong culture for it. There is something about the warrior lifestyle that I have always found attractive. In my imagination, the closest thing that I could see myself as was a kind of Samurai figure. I think of how they single-mindedly trained and trained, and became really good at their craft; that is how I see myself. I think of myself as being that warrior figure and a role model for other women of color in the sport of climbing.

The Spirit and Nature

As far as my spirituality or religion goes, I would say I get it from my yoga and my connection to nature. The physical movements of yoga offer opportunity for meditation. The way my brain works, I seem to be able to get to that level of calmness and insight through yoga and rock climbing and do not feel the need to have a figure or icon represent that for me. I have been to churches as a young person, but I never felt that it really helped me get closer to anything spiritual. That interpretation just never worked for me. I feel more of a sense of spirituality in the outdoors, and one of my favorite places for that is Cathedral Peak in Yosemite. I get an incredible sense of spirituality there.

Minorities in Our Wild Places

I led a women-of-color trip for wild women workshops last year, but this year we did not get enough participants. That really saddened me. I had hoped that getting a group of women of color to go into the outdoors would have also contributed to getting kids of color out as well. I put up flyers all over San Francisco, but it was still hard to find any women at all who were interested. I shamelessly stopped women in the streets or who were riding bicycles,

The 3,000-foot vertical wall of El Capitan, Yosemite National Park

asking them if they were interested. I even went to women-of-color conferences, trying to get the word out about our outdoor workshops. After that, I kind of ran out of ideas to encourage more interest.

I am not sure that many women of color know that the outdoors is even available to them. With so many women leading such stressful lives, raising children or just working their butts off out there, nature offers a much-needed break. I talk to a lot of women around town and they say, "You know, I would really love to do that sometime, but I have kids and my job and all of these responsibilities." I think if they really thought it was important they could get some of those things covered for them long enough to get out there and take that break. They probably are thinking, "You know, this is kind of a weird thing and I don't know anyone else doing it." I want to bring the awareness of the value of taking the time to be in the outdoors to women of color, and I wish I could find other people who are interested in doing that with me.

Best Outdoor Experiences and Favorite Places

My favorite places to spend time outdoors are Yosemite National Park and Joshua Tree National Monument. I have lots of friends in those areas, and it is nice to visit and climb with them. I also love to climb the Needles area in the southern Sierra Nevada Mountains of California. It is an incredibly beautiful area with just tons and tons of cool climbing to do. I enjoy checking out new areas, too, but some of those classic climbs, like the ones in the Nevadas, I could just do over and over again and never get tired of them. If a climb is considered a "classic climb" by climbers, there is usually a reason for it, and once you climb it you say, "Oh, I see why that is now."

I have had so many memorable experiences outdoors, partly because in climbing you can get to places that are not accessible any other way. For instance, sleeping on a tiny ledge on the face of El Capitan in Yosemite Park, maybe 2,000 feet above the valley floor, is a mind-blowing experience. To get a visual of what that is like, imagine climbing on the outside of a 3,000-foot skyscraper, and about two-thirds of the way up you have to sleep overnight on a window ledge until the next morning. That is something at one time I thought I would have never been able to do. People ask me, "How can you relax? How can you sleep?" I mean, when evening comes and you are still at least 1,000 feet from the summit on a 3,000-foot vertical granite rock face, you have to sleep somewhere. You are happy to find a place you can sit still for several hours and feel the breeze go by, or watch the sunset or the moonrise. It is just good to be able to rest and collect your thoughts after a long day of climbing.

Environmental Advocacy and the Future

We have a responsibility to our environment in terms of recycling, reusing, and reducing waste. We, as mass consumers, accumulate so much packaging and stuff, and then we throw it away. The question I have is, "Where is 'away?'" It is not like that garbage disappears and goes to a better place; someone somewhere will have to deal with it. If people would make better choices when they buy things—to purchase products with less packaging or buy more products in bulk—and send that message back to manufacturers about the waste that is built into their products, that would be a step in the right direction towards being environmentally responsible people. Even little choices we make every day, like bringing your own to-go mug to a fast-food restaurant, can make a big difference.

Chelsea lives in Oakland, California. In 2001, she became the first Black woman to climb world-famous El Capitan in Yosemite National Park. She is a well-known free climber and still occasionally volunteers at Bay Area Wilderness Training in Oakland, an organization that aims to make the outdoors more accessible to low-income and BIPOC youth.

Unfortunately, Chelsea was diagnosed with multiple sclerosis a few years ago and is unable to climb any longer. Nonetheless, Chelsea's long career in the climbing world has inspired so many women of color across the country. She is a true role model and trailblazer in the sport.

—Dudley Edmondson

BY 1957, MY MOTHER HAD 10 children. Five boys and five girls—a very poor woman living in the South, in the Mississippi River Delta. She was looking for one child to break the tie, but also looking for that one baby who she would take fishing with her. It was September in Arkansas and the Little Rock Nine were all over the news and on the radio. My mother was very impressed at the way President Eisenhower had handled the situation, using the military to escort the children into Central High School. She was so impressed that she decided she would have a little boy. She said, "I am going to name him Ike, and I am going to take him fishing with me." A little more than a month later, I was born on Ike's birthday, October 14, but, of course, I was a girl. So my mother named me Mamie, after the president's wife.

Childhood Experiences and Turning Points in Nature

My mother always made me feel special and always called me "the first lady." She told me, "I hope that you will do a lot of things in your life as a first lady." At the time, of course, I had no idea what she meant. She followed through on her pledge to take me fishing, and fishing became our special time together.

In our family, fishing was more than about recreation; it was also about putting protein on our dinner table. For me, fishing on those riverbanks with my mother became a place to learn life lessons. My mother only had an eighth-grade education, but she was very intelligent and a great philosopher. On top of that, she was an avid angler. I call her "Oprah of the Outdoors," because people were always coming to her for advice. Mama loved poetry as well. She shared many of

MAMIE PARKER

Assistant Director of Fisheries and Habitat Conservation, U.S. Fish and Wildlife Service Washington, D.C.

her favorite poems and poets, introducing me to Emily Dickinson—"I dwell in Possibility."

The schools in Little Rock were integrated when I was born, but it took until the third grade before my little town in southern Arkansas would fully embrace it. Many people fought for that to happen, including my mother, but when it came time to send the Black kids to the white school, many parents were afraid. They did not know for sure if their children would be safe there. So one day the principal from the nearby Black school came by our house and neighborhood, talking to different parents, trying to ease their minds and encourage them to send their kids to the white school. They came to our house and talked to my mother, saying, "You know, your daughter is really smart and she will do well in that environment." They were trying to get my sister to come, because she was two years older. My mother said, "No, I think I will send my baby girl, because she can talk her way out of anything." So I was one of the first to integrate white schools in my hometown.

That was the beginning of my journey as a "first lady," just like my mom told me I would be. It was a real eye opener, as I had spent all of my life until then in a very secure African American community of people that were very loving, caring, and strong-willed. That environment, like fishing with my mother, sort of insulated me from the rest of the world. I had no idea that it would prepare me for my future and living in other parts of the country, in places like Minnesota and Wisconsin, where the minority populations in the rural communities in which I lived were much smaller.

Mamie's mother back home in Arkansas

At the integrated school I attended, we did have some unspoken boundaries, and you did not talk to white kids off the school grounds, or on the way home, or even at the grocery store; it was just uncommon, at least in my hometown of Wilmot, Arkansas, where I grew up picking cotton and whatever else we could pick.

So during my time at the white school, I did not have a lot of friends in the area to play with, and that made it easier for me to continue going fishing with my mama. I also believe that because I went fishing I never became a teen mother, and I am very thankful for that.

The one commonality of living in southwestern Wisconsin and the Deep South was the great Mississippi River. Whenever I got homesick, I would just go down to the river, and that was always a good feeling.

As a high school student, I was really impressed with my science teacher, who was also an outdoor person. He liked to hunt and talked a lot about it, and I really looked up to him. His passion for science and the outdoors helped affirm mine. So when I went to college, I decided to major in biology, not knowing there was an opportunity for a career.

What I Do in the Outdoors

One day when I was in college, I had gone fishing and returned to discover staff from the university were looking for me. Hannibal Bolton, who worked for the U.S. Fish and Wildlife Service, was recruiting minorities to come and work for the organization. He was like a used-car salesman, and he sold me on the Service idea. By the time he was done talking I was like, "Of course I will take the position. That sounds like the fun place to be." He led me to believe it was somewhere in Arkansas, but I later discovered that the job was in Wisconsin. When I called him up and asked, "Isn't it very cold in Wisconsin?" He said, "Yes, it can be." And like a used-car salesman, he told me, "Let me see what I can do." He called me back and said, "I tell you what, we will throw in some clothes for you." Those clothes turned out to be a Service uniform, and everybody who worked for them got them free. Just like a car salesman, I did not see him again after that for many years, but now he works for me. He was really passionate about the Service, and he really pulled me into it.

I really enjoyed working and fishing in Wisconsin and Minnesota. The one commonality of living in southwestern Wisconsin and the Deep South was the great Mississippi River. Whenever I got homesick, I would just go down to the river, and that was always a good feeling. I had a lot of Fish and

Wildlife jobs in the upper Midwest. In Wisconsin, I got introduced to ice fishing and enjoyed that a lot. In Missouri, I learned some different things about the outdoors and got involved in what we now call the Partners for Fish and Wildlife program. That program involved working with land-owners to get them to convert farms to land that would protect or increase wildlife populations. So I got introduced to pheasant, quail, and turkey hunting, and really enjoyed working with farmers there.

I lived in Atlanta, Georgia, for a while before moving here to D.C. Shortly after moving to Atlanta, I was at a point in my life when I was thinking of leaving the Fish and Wildlife Service and looking for a teaching job at a university. I got a call from the director's office here and they wanted me to come in and become the Special Assistant to the Deputy Director of the agency. That was another one of those "first lady" things my mama talked about—at that time no minority had done that. I tore up my letter of resignation from the Service and took that job. The first day I stuck the key in the door of my new office as the Special Assistant to the Deputy Director, I realized that no other African American had stuck a key in that

A bend in the Mississippi River

door other than to clean that office as a janitor. That really hit me hard. Ms. Mary Bethune, an African American woman of many accomplishments in education for minority women in the early 1900s, said, "Lift as we climb," meaning it is up to those who succeed in life to bring others up with them. So that when we turn around and look in life, there are others following in our footsteps.

I stayed in that job for a few years and then had the opportunity to move to Massachusetts. Another "first lady" moment came there when I became the Deputy Regional Director for the 13 northeastern states. I stayed in that job for four years before I got another call from the director of the agency in 2003. This time I was asked to return to D.C. and be the Assistant Director of the agency. That was another first for a minority.

My job title now is Assistant Director of Fisheries and Habitat Conservation. The facilities include 70 National Fish Hatcheries, 64 Fishery Resource Offices, 9 Fish Health Centers, 7 Fish Technology Centers, and over 50 Ecological Services Offices. We also have one genetic lab

A green darner dragonfly lays eggs in a pond.

and one historic hatchery. I set guidance and policy for about 2,400 employees throughout the nation. There is an enormous sense of responsibility and duty that comes with my job, and I take it very seriously. Being the first African American female in many of the job titles I have held with the Service, I do take it very seriously indeed. It is not something I want to brag about, but it does mean I have a lot of people looking up to me and that is what motivates me to want to do more and be the best I can at what I do.

Heroes and Mentors

I have many heroes and mentors, including my mother, my husband, and my siblings, but two of the more famous ones are Maya Angelou and Oprah Winfrey. When I sit on the riverbanks fishing, I take them with me in spirit. That is something I learned from reading former President John Adams's writings, when he said, "If you have a poet in your pocket, you are never alone." So those are my ladies, and Maya is a fellow Arkansan, which is neat too. I would have to say that any leader that stepped out and was courageous enough to go against conventional wisdom stands out in my mind. You can name many African Americans and women that have done that. But what is really important is that they stood up for what they believed in even when everybody was badmouthing them. Jesus Christ is my hero and that is OK. He certainly fits the bill, standing alone and standing on principles and believing in something. Even in the Bible it talks about being great stewards of our kingdom. Most environmentalists are my heroes, too, because they are eternal optimists. Think about it—you plant a tree and you know it will be at least 40 years before that tree is really ready for any type of wildlife that would benefit from it. Also, it is being optimistic to believe that the world can be a better place, thinking ahead to future generations of both animals and humans.

Minorities in Our Wild Places

I don't think minorities spend enough time in the outdoors, but I think it is the fear of the unknown and a lack of access and success. That is a big issue right now and we don't talk a lot about it, but many people of color can't get there—they can't drive to wherever; it is not that easy for them. I think about that all the time.

I think having more minority heroes and heroes in these fields of study and seeing that it is OK to enjoy the outdoors will help. I got teased a lot growing up because I liked the outdoors, and it is always hard going against peer pressure. All we need to do is get someone that people look up to, to say that it is cool for African American kids to like the outdoors, then things will change, but right now we just don't have enough of those types of role models to pull in young people. I know there are a lot of celebrities and sports stars that are doing it. I know there are a lot of football players out there who love fishing. But we need more people in the spotlight who enjoy nature so these kids can relate to people that look like them and think like them.

Best Outdoor Experiences and Favorite Places

I remember sitting on the banks of Lake Enterprise in southeast Arkansas with my mama one day. That was the first time we ever went fishing together. I picked up a Coca-Cola bottle from the mud and said, "Look, Mama, I can read!" She said, "What does it say, baby?" I told her, "No deposit, no return." And she said, "There is a life lesson in there." She said,

"You have to make investments in yourself and others in order to get something back in life." I must have caught bass and bluegill that day, but it is not the fish I remember so much; it is the life lessons I learned that stand out the most in my mind from that special day with my mama. I have never forgotten them.

Being a Face of Color in Remote Places

I have gone to national wildlife refuges and they ask me if they can help me, thinking I am lost. Perhaps the assumption is that you must be looking for something else, because you can't be here for enjoyment of wildlife, looking for birds, or a fishing spot, or whatever. I think when anyone, no matter who they are or what their race, arrives, you should just make them feel welcome. I know the refuge system is working on this. I don't think it is done intentionally all the time, but perhaps it is just so new to them that they just have not figured out how to respond to it yet.

Environmental Advocacy and the Future

I still think as people we can always do a bit more in our lives. There is a poem I share with people and it goes, "Each day I live I want to be a day to give the best of me. / I'm only one but not alone, / my finest day is yet unknown." My mother died when I was very young, and every time I think about giving up, I think of the words of that poem, and basically that makes me think about her. Her words to me about "keep going and growing" were one of the last things she said to me on the day she died. A part of us will always listen to our mothers, so I think that is what we have to do as environmentalists, keep going and growing. Our finest day is yet unknown.

Mamie left the USFWS, where she was the first Black American Regional Director and later the Head of Fisheries. She then rewired and is now a well-sought-after executive coach and public speaker and sits on a number of advisory boards. Mamie has always been a trailblazer, from her experience in the segregated South to later becoming the first Black chair of the Virginia Department of Wildlife Resource Commission, and she was even inducted into the Arkansas Outdoor Hall of Fame. She continues to promote and mentor women and people of color in outdoor careers.

—Dudley Edmondson

HUNTING IS NOT ALWAYS ABOUT KILLING an animal. I know there have been many times when that opportunity came and I just let the animal walk on by; I did not want to kill. That is a choice you can make as a hunter—you can choose to just enjoy being in that animal's presence and not kill it. The sporting part of it is finding that animal, tracking it, and being prepared to kill it if you choose to.

Childhood Experiences and Turning Points in Nature

I have been involved in the outdoors all of my life. I grew up in the inner city (at least that is what I called it) in West Palm Beach County, Florida, just 24 miles north of Fort Lauderdale, in the 1970s. We had a pretty high crime rate, just like most other Black communities, and most of the typical problems of inner-city neighborhoods all across the country.

My father was from Alabama, and he grew up around mules and farm life, and they hunted rabbits and raccoons and opossums. When they hunted, it was to put food on the table. Not that they were starving, but it was just a way of life that he knew. When he came to Florida, he kind of brought that with him. He also bought cattle, which was something that he had always wanted. So we kids got the chance to be around herds of beef cattle and horses. My brother and I, along with all the other young boys in the neighborhood, kind of looked up to my father. He was like a magnet—all the kids wanted to go with my dad to tend to the cattle and horses on his 40 acres of land.

My father was also a heavy equipment operator in undeveloped parts of Florida, building roads and stuff. Most of the areas he worked in were out

HANK WILLIAMS JR.

**Big-Game Hunter and Black Cowboy
Rush City, Minnesota**

in the middle of nowhere, so we got to go with him on weekends to work. My dad would get on his big piece of machinery and we would take out our little pellet guns and go exploring the woods. Every little bird we saw was at risk, so my father was very serious when he said, "Everything you kill, you have to eat, so think before you shoot." So if we killed a crow or something, we said, "OK, now we have to pluck it, cook it, and eat it." It was fun feeling like we were outdoorsmen.

That was my exposure to the outdoors, wandering around the woods with my pellet gun. I must have been about 13 or 15 years old then. That interest in the outdoors just grew and grew along with me.

What I Do in the Outdoors

Hunting is the big thing for me, and big game is the most fun. That means elk, deer, bear—those kinds of animals. Discovering new areas and all the research involved in that, and talking with local hunters all add an element of excitement for me. Being outside in different landscapes is also very exciting to me.

Off-season, I enjoy firearms. I remember in my upbringing I heard that guns were something to hurt people with, because that is the way they are portrayed on television, that people buy guns to protect themselves. I do not see guns that way. To me they are no different than a golf club or a football—they are simply one crucial element in a sport, and that sport is hunting. So I am a gun enthusiast. I love guns that use black powder cartridges, guns made in the 1800s. They are a lot slower, a lot more difficult to shoot, and they require a lot more knowledge to use them skillfully, to acquire the accuracy capable of dispatching game.

Horses are another big thing of mine in the off-season. I enjoy roping and riding. I enjoy working with these animals. They are athletes, but on a different level. They will require you to step up your physical abilities just to be able to work with them. So when you work with horses in a competition, you are not only competing against other riders, but against their horses as well. I just bought 32 acres of land here in northern Minnesota, and I am building a new house, horse stables, and a riding-and-roping arena. All of my roping friends are white who live in my community. I know there are other Black ropers around the country, but we are kind of scattered. I would like to help others learn about the sport in the future. I already have a young Black student who is the daughter of my best friend. I started out showing her older brother how to throw a rope, and when she saw it she became interested. It turned out he never really took a liking to it and gave it up, but she really wanted to learn more, so I work with her on it, and she is coming along real nice.

Camping is another thing I enjoy, along with fishing and anything that puts me in the outdoors that requires my physical and mental attention.

Storm clouds over a California valley

Heroes and Mentors

As far as mentors and heroes go, I would have to say that my father fills both. I really did not know any other adult males as well as him. I was around others in church and stuff, but it was my father who just did the kinds of things I liked doing. We would go horseback riding or get on tractors and go out into the woods; he was just play. He bought my brother and me pellet guns, even though Mom said, "Don't get those boys them guns." He did it, but he set down rules for us, and then he let us explore the world around us. So he was everything to me.

Today too many kids look up to adult males they see on TV, and that is very sad, I think. These kids are looking for mentors, and for many the best they can find is a celebrity on TV. Fortunately for my brother and me, my father was right there, and all the other boys in the neighborhood liked hanging out with him too. On the weekends they would be hanging off his truck, wanting to go with us. And my father would have to say, "I can't take all of you," but he would try it anyways. I think every kid that my father took out to work with the horses and cattle are still into the outdoors.

The Spirit and Nature

I would say my favorite place is the frame of mind I am in once I am in the woods. You do what you need to do for the next step, and then sometimes there is a quiet moment, and in those quiet spaces you think about things you may not always talk about with other people, you know, personal things. You think about God, you think about personal achievements, about trying harder to be the person you want to be. I always say my God lives in the treetops, because as a hunter I spend a lot of time sitting up in trees watching and waiting for game. I say that because that is where I spend a lot of Sundays. I do believe in God, and I think he understands me. They say he knows all, so I think he must know why I am out here; it is just who I am. When I am out there in the trees, I am at peace and I am contemplating how to be a better person.

I will not allow anybody to deny me my right to go out and enjoy the outdoors. It's like denying me the right to vote; it is that important to me.

Minorities in Our Wild Places

I don't think we spend enough time in the outdoors. We tend to think of certain aspects of city life as a vacation. Going to a nice hotel is a vacation. Visiting a major city, like Chicago, is a vacation. Not that there is anything wrong with those places, but I never hear any of my people talk about going to Yellowstone or the Grand Tetons as a vacation destination.

I often ask when I see Black hunters in my travels, usually local folks in local areas, if they want to travel to other parts of the country to hunt elk or something. In most cases they are only interested in hunting near home, in areas they know. Going out of their communities to hunt is not something they want to do, and I see the same thing for Black people and vacationing—they go where they know, not wanting to travel to places like national parks or wilderness areas.

Youth and Wilderness

The outdoors offers adults the opportunity to get their kids' attention. In the inner city, there are a lot of distractions, but in the outdoors it is just you and that individual, and you can talk one on one. A lot can be taught and learned in that environment. My father is 74 now, and he and I still look forward to going hunting together.

There should also be a major effort to tell history truthfully. Black history is so incomplete right now, there are so many pieces that most kids were never taught in school. Blacks played a big role in the westward expansion of the United States as pioneering explorers, entrepreneurs, and cowboys like Bill Pickett, but few kids learn that in their history lessons. Once those contributions become part of the curriculum, perhaps Black youth may take more interest in the outdoors.

Best Outdoor Experiences and Favorite Places

One outing that stands out in my mind involved bear hunting. I was up in my bear stand one fall, and after a while I saw a fairly large bear, maybe 400 or so pounds, appear at the edge of the woods. The bear did not come in too close. I had put out bait, but it just stayed on the perimeter. I thought to myself, "Something is different here, this bear is acting a bit unusual." After a while it came in closer to the bait. It still did not come all the way in, but it did get a little closer. Then after a while, one little bear cub appears and pops out of the woods, then another, until there were four cubs!

Now most sows will have three in a year, but she had four. So I watched them eat the bait and she just hung back and kept an eye out. The four little cubs came in and filled their little bellies so much they were dragging on the ground. Anytime there was a little noise in the woods, it would send them running up a tree until the sow would give them the OK to come back down and feed.

Needless to say, I never shot her. I watched her and her cubs for two years. They sure were fun to watch. I would just take pictures of them running around wrestling with each other. I took it upon myself to take care of her and her cubs, and I think I did a pretty good job. Then in the third season she did not come back anymore. I figured now her cubs were two or three years old, so they were on their own and she had probably moved on to a different territory.

Being a Face of Color in Remote Places

I have run into some racial prejudice in the outdoors, and I have met some really nice folks out there too. The amount of racism that you may run into in the outdoors is equal to the amount of racism that you will run into in the city or anywhere else you may travel in this country, as far as I am concerned. Bottom line is, I am not going to let anyone anywhere stop me from enjoying these resources that I know are partly mine anyway. The outdoors belongs to all of us. I will not allow anybody to deny me my right to go out and enjoy the outdoors. It's like denying me the right to vote; it is that important to me.

Environmental Advocacy and the Future

I don't think, personally, that Blacks have an agenda for the outdoors. When I talk to my people, they don't seem to have an awareness of the benefits and the importance of it. Their focus seems to be on inner-city life. I won't say I know the reason for that definitely, but I can speculate about the reasons. I would say partly because their role models have no interest in the outdoors.

Right now just the mention of the outdoors seems like a bad thing in the minds of African Americans. I guess I will go ahead and say it, but it reminds our people of slavery times when life was hard. The economic foundation of this country was built on free slave labor, and that is a very painful part of our history. When you talk about the outdoors to today's generation, it

A wary doe peers into a northern Minnesota forest on a cold winter day.

seems to them as a step backwards to those times. Progress to our people sounds like or looks like or comes in the form of excessive wealth, concrete-and-steel high-rise buildings, and new automobiles, but has nothing to do with the outdoors.

Our national parks require funding from the government to maintain. As minority populations in this country increase, we will have more political power. I think our people have a sympathetic heart towards wildlife species, but our awareness of their needs is not as great as it should be. If African Americans and other minorities had the majority vote today, I think funding would go more towards city infrastructure and not towards wilderness protection.

I think it is very important for everyone to try to further the Black community's interest in the outdoors, so I have developed an organization called the Black Outdoor Sportsman Network, or BOSN. We are a networking resource for Black sportsmen and women so they can find places and other people to enjoy the outdoors with. The organization's goal is to provide education to youths about the outdoors, as well as sharing hunting techniques and even wild-game recipes.

Hank still lives in Rush City, Minnesota, on his land. He's in the computer technology business but still enjoys things from the past, including 19th-century weapons, like black powder cartridge rifles. He says it takes more skill to hunt big game with these less-accurate guns. He still enjoys the cowboy life and participates in team cattle-roping competitions.

—Dudley Edmondson

I AM THE EXECUTIVE DIRECTOR OF the Gunflint Trail Association in northeastern Minnesota. The Gunflint is a vacation destination for people from around the region and the world. The 57-mile paved highway goes north out of Grand Marais, Minnesota, through some of the most beautiful wilderness area you may ever see, and turns west, ending on Saganaga Lake near the Canadian border. People visit the trail to access the Boundary Waters Canoe Area. There is so much to do off the Gunflint at anytime of the year, including fishing, camping, and hiking—and skiing in the winter. You can watch wildlife at all times of the year. Moose, bears, wolves, deer, and a host of other cool animals make the area their home. The best part about my job is telling tourists how to have fun in a place that I love.

By most people's standards, Grand Marais would seem very remote. Most of what we do here is outdoors. Closest movie theater or shopping mall is 75 miles away. I tell people, "There is Lake Superior, it's right there in front of you. It is the largest freshwater lake in the world, and you can't find anything to do?"

Childhood Experiences and Turning Points in Nature

As a child growing up in Chicago, Illinois, in the Lake Meadows area, I got to experience a lot of Chicago's Lake Michigan waterfront and some of the parks there.

My father's parents lived on a farm near Alton, Illinois, close to St. Louis, until their deaths, so we were at the farm quite a bit. My father and my grandfather and uncles would be on tractors, so I would be out there watching them work or following them around. It was a working farm— cows, chickens, horses, and pigs. They raised most

JUDIE JOHNSON

Executive Director, Gunflint Trail Association
Grand Marais, Minnesota

Judie at Gooseberry Falls State Park on the shores
of Lake Superior, north of Two Harbors, Minnesota   **119**

A view from the 200-foot cliffs along the North Shore above Lake Superior in Minnesota inside Tettegouche State Park

of their food. We got to do all those living-off-the-land things that most kids don't get to do. The area where my grandparents' farm was is still a little wild, but with urban sprawl I think it will all be gone in a decade or so, which is kind of sad.

Our family took vacations a lot during my childhood, which a lot of Blacks did not get to do back then. We would go for two to three weeks. We would camp and stay in hotels. My sister and I read *National Geographic,* so we would plan vacations using information in them. We traveled all over. We were a curious family, wanting to see things we had never seen before—my parents nurtured that.

One year we took a trip from Chicago across the country to Yellowstone National Park, the Painted Desert, Mesa Verde National Park, and a few other places. We visited my father's brother and my mother's aunt in L.A. Then we went up the coast and camped at Big Sur. Then we went to the Hearst Castle of W. Randolph Hearst, the millionaire, in San Simeon. There was a Black guy there who was a tour guide and he gave us a private tour, so that was pretty cool. After that, we went up to San Francisco. From there we stopped at Yellowstone, the Tetons, then through the Badlands of the Dakotas, eventually making our way back to Chicago. We stayed at a lot of national parks and some state parks.

On another trip we visited Lake Louise in Jasper, Canada, then went out on the Athabaska Glacier. I was so excited that my heart was going a mile a minute when we got out of the snow tracker, the vehicle that they take you out on the glacier in. They told us all about the formation of the glacier. As the guide was talking, I could see, over in the distance, there was a group of people. So I told my father, "Let's go see who they are." So we went over, and I was pleased to find out it was none other than a *National Geographic* magazine crew out working on an upcoming project. So I, of course, was extremely excited, to say the least. I got to talk with them and find out what they did and why they were over there. They sent me a special reprint of that copy of the magazine, which was really cool.

A wilderness experience gives kids new opportunities, and it is exposure, in the same sense that a child should be exposed to the arts and sciences. Whether or not it becomes something they choose to master is up to them, but they should be allowed to make a choice.

What I Do in the Outdoors

I actually bought land here, knowing that someday I wanted to move here. One day I was sitting at home in Minneapolis trolling their local paper and there was the Gunflint Trail Association director job. I thought to myself, "OK, by the time I am ready to move up there, something like this is bound to come up open again." So my sister called me on the last day they were accepting applications for that job and said, "If you don't apply, I will get an old copy of your résumé and send it in." I said, "OK, fine," and I faxed in a current version of my résumé to the office. I got a call within a few hours of sending the fax. Long story short, they made me an offer. So I accepted the job.

I remembered my mother telling me that, when I was 10 years old, I returned from a summer camp in Wisconsin and announced that I was moving to the woods when I grew up. So when I moved up here to Grand Marais, it was no shock to her. I am pretty sure I am the only Black woman living in the whole town. People asked my mom, "What is wrong with Judie?" And she told them, "Judie told me she was moving to the woods a long time ago, and now she has finally done it."

Heroes and Mentors

My grandparents and parents were my mentors and heroes. My grandmother raised chickens, and sometimes a fox or weasel would get into the chicken coop and she could tell by the sound the chickens were making as to which predator was in the coop. I have seen my grandmother standing at the sink washing dishes and she would stop, dry her hands on her apron, and there was a corner closet by the back door where she would keep a shotgun. She would get the shotgun, step out on the back steps, flip the porch light on, and wait for the animal to come out of the chicken coop. My grandmother rarely missed a shot that I can remember. She would come back in the house after killing the varmint and send one of the menfolk out back to go and dispose of the dead animal. As a little girl, I thought, "Grandma is really cool! You go, Grandma!" Oh yeah, Grandma was bad!

Violets have a special meaning to me, because as a little girl my grandmother and I used to go down to the woods by the creek and we would dig up violets. I would move the violets up to the house and plant them up there in my grandmother's front yard. When we moved to Minnesota from Illinois, I brought a patch of violets from my grandmother's with me and planted them in my mother's yard. And then when I moved up here to Grand Marais, I dug up a patch from my mother's house and planted them up here. She took violets from Minnesota back to the farm in Illinois, and that is my connection to my grandmother even now.

Minorities in Our Wild Places

You know I don't think anyone spends enough time in the outdoors— African Americans or whoever—with the exception of a few fortunate people. The idea of going out and playing or working in the woods is just not something many Americans in general aspire to do, and even fewer Blacks. It is just not a mainstream activity in Black culture. For Blacks, moving away from the South to the North, it was out of necessity, in search of industrial jobs and getting away from the slavery culture. I don't think we African Americans as a group have an outdoor culture anymore. We are so focused on trying to get a piece of the American dream.

A view of a distant lake from the Mt. Oberg Trail along the North Shore of Lake Superior in Minnesota

You know, people talk about the lack of disposable income to pursue outdoor interests being a factor, but these days the Black middle class has grown substantially, so I am not so sure that is a big factor anymore. There is also the fear of the unknown, which is probably more the case, but I think that can be overcome with education about the environment. However, with the scarcity of Blacks in the outdoors, there is the bigger fear of being the only one out there, and then thoughts of violence from racial prejudice come into play.

Youth and Wilderness

After I got out of college with a degree in Chinese history and a minor in English and biochemistry, I worked in youth camps in the summer and discovered how comfortable I was in the woods, and how it was a necessity in my life.

Regardless of a kid's background, there seems to be a sense of wonderment as well as fear when they are out in nature initially. Then, as time passes, they develop a certain amount of self-assurance from the experience. Watching the detachment and resentment from a kid for expecting them to do something for themselves, like pitch a tent so they have a place to sleep that night, is very interesting. They look at you like, "Hey, I don't know how to do that. You are supposed to do it for me!" I tell them, "I will be glad to show you how to do it, dear, but you will have to do it yourself." Their attitude changes as we work together to get the job done. They realize they can do something they had no idea they were capable of. In the wilderness, you have to be able to appreciate and absorb what is around you, then you have to exercise creativity in what you do.

Being in the wilderness gives you a sense of place in the world. You recognize that the world is bigger than you. A wilderness experience gives kids new opportunities, and it is exposure, in the same sense that a child should be exposed to the arts and sciences. Whether or not it becomes something they choose to master is up to them, but they should be allowed to make a choice. It is something they probably don't know is a possibility; and yes, you can get paid to do it. No, you will not make the kind of money a company CEO or sports star or rapper makes, but you can get a living wage with a more enjoyable, less-stressed life.

Best Outdoor Experiences and Favorite Places

My favorite outdoor activity depends on the time of year. I love skiing. It doesn't matter if it's cross-country, downhill, or telemark. I enjoy riding my mountain bike, rock climbing, trail running, swimming in freshwater, canoeing, and kayaking. My favorite activity is always whatever I am doing at that moment until I can do the next thing. It's fun to combine activities like canoeing and rock climbing in the same day on one trip! Those are great days because you put so much of yourself into them and so you sleep like a zombie at night.

Traveling abroad gave me a unique perspective on how people in other cultures live. When I was in China and Peru, the animals that were found in the street markets were an eye opener to me. Seeing things that you knew were endangered species for sale really shocked me. OK, you know poaching and other illegal acts happen intellectually, but seeing it right at arm's length is very different.

The lost city of Machu Picchu on the Inca Trail in Peru is a very spiritual and sacred place. There is a place at Machu Picchu where the sun comes through the stone perfectly during the spring equinox. There is a mountain above Machu Picchu called Jaguar, and when you climb up there you understand everything. I understood why Machu Picchu was built there. And I had also studied the Great Wall of China for quite a while in college, so when I stood on it, I understood completely why they built it. You could see forever.

Being a Face of Color in Remote Places

One year I was camping in the Boundary Waters Canoe Area with my mother and sister when we met a park ranger. He came over and chatted with us and did his official job checking out our permit. My mother, like many mothers, is one of those people that can get a total stranger's complete life story; people just feel comfortable talking to her. So I thought, "This is great! My mother actually got to meet a park ranger and see him work and stuff."

So he had been looking at our gear and finally he asked me, "Who outfitted you guys? Where did you get your gear?" I said, "Out of my basement and garage. Why?" He looked at me with curiosity and asked if he could take our picture, and I said, "Why?" My mother and my sister are kind of looking at him and he said, "It is just that I have never seen three Black women in the wilderness by themselves before. Most of the time I see just one or two Blacks in the group, so I have never seen anything like you before." That, to me, is not prejudice, per se. That is plain ignorance and curiosity.

There are times when I get tired of educating people and satisfying people's curiosity. There are times when I find it amusing. You know, he is right, and I know I am an anomaly. Trust me, I know. I have been out there and I have not seen many people that look like me. But you know, I am not sure I would walk up to a white person and say, "You know, I have never seen someone like you in this neighborhood before." Because, basically, that is what he said. It is not good, bad, or indifferent—it is unfortunate. It is unfortunate in the sense that his statement is true; it is unfortunate in the sense that there are so many opportunities for people to interact with nature; it is unfortunate that it is the first time this man, a full-time year-round ranger who obviously spends more time in nature than I do, has come across a group of Black women. The skills and talents that I have developed I acquired by being there in the outdoors. Yes, I recognize that

Mountain range in Glacier National Park

that makes me unique, but it is also very unfortunate that the outdoors is an educational opportunity that my contemporaries have missed.

Environmental Advocacy and the Future

We should all be concerned about the environment and the neighborhoods we live in. People who live in low-income neighborhoods should be very concerned about the environmental waste and air quality where they live. When I moved to Dearborn, Michigan, many years back, I called the EPA and asked them, "OK, where do I not want to live?" And they said, "What do you mean?" I said, "It is very simple, this is 'Auto Industry, U.S.A.,' and I have concerns about what kind of ground runoff there is and what might seep into my home, etc." They said, "OK, in this section of the city we send out advisories after every rainstorm not to walk in the streets because of the pollutants that are in the rainwater, and in different areas the time frames are longer than others." The longest time frame for these advisories happened to be in the traditionally Black neighborhoods in the inner city. In some of the suburban areas, the EPA or some company would go in and clean up the area, particularly if it would later become a neighborhood that would house some of their employees. That does not occur in all communities. Traditional areas of housing for people of color are usually marginal.

Judie has retired from the Gunflint Trail Association, which is now part of Visit Cook County. While she continues to enjoy all the county has to offer, she's frequently traveling to the wild places of the world, learning about culture, traditions, and histories.

—*Dudley Edmondson*

I GOT INTO NATURE IN AN odd kind of way. I was not the brightest student in the class. I will not lie to you—I was straight-up lazy. I can remember it plain as day. I was sitting with my folks just after my sister had graduated from college; I had just graduated from high school. We were sitting there talking about what I was going to do and if I wanted to continue into college. Well, I did not want to go to college. They said, "Son, you are going to have to do something, what about forestry?" I said, "Why would I want to do that?" They said, "Because not many minorities are in the field!" I said, "Well, Blacks don't do that kind of work." My father said, "And that is a bonus in your favor."

I eventually decided on the military, and I served down at Fort Campbell, in Kentucky, which was a short distance from where my entire family was from. I loved the Army, refueling helicopters and stuff, and just enjoyed being out-of-doors.

I stayed in the Army for five years and enjoyed it. After that, I really wanted to get back into law enforcement, so I did corrections first, and enjoyed that. Then this job came along. It was the perfect setting, because I love being outdoors. As a full-time ranger in law enforcement, I had to go to a police academy and graduate. I graduated third in my class. I was one of the class officers. Unfortunately, I did not have the formal training most of my colleagues have; I did not go to school for forestry, which would have put me on par with most of the other students in my graduating class.

Childhood Experiences and Turning Points in Nature

Much of my summer as a kid was spent going back to Kentucky and my uncles' farms. I would go down and help out. I learned how to drive

MARSHALL REESE

**Assistant Park Manager and Ranger,
Franklin County Metropolitan Park System
Columbus, Ohio**

a tractor at my uncles', learned to mow at my uncles', slopped hogs and milked cows, all at my uncles' houses. They lived just near Hopkinsville, in Christian County.

My folks were typical Black parents of that time, so when school got out, they said, "Go outside and play. Get exercise. Ride your bike. Do something, but don't sit around the house all day." As long as my parents knew where I was, I was fine. Lunch was at 11:30 a.m., so you came home, ate lunch on time, and then remembered dinner was at 3 p.m., so you needed to be home by then. So my folks made sure we all got outside and played.

The only other reason we might not be in Kentucky in the summer was because we were away at some type of church sport camp. My folks were big believers that everybody needs to play some type of sport to stay in shape. They felt it was important not only for the exercise but for the interaction with other kids, both Black and white, so you learn how to get along and

Lush deciduous woodland

work with other people. We went to those camps every year from about the time I was 8 until I was 12 years old. We learned a lot of things, from wilderness survival skills to plant and tree identification.

My parents' investment in getting me into the outdoors paid off in me becoming a park ranger. They knew I liked the outdoors and they did everything they could to keep me on the right track by structuring and nurturing my interests.

What I Do in the Outdoors

My official title here is Assistant Park Manager with the Franklin County Metro Park Systems of Columbus, Ohio, serving at Sharon Woods Metro Park. My job here is the same as the manager's job. If the manager is not here, I run the park. If he is here and is too busy doing paperwork, I run the park. I can also decide to come in today and put on a maintenance uniform and go brush some trails or mow and repair something.

We do have weapons, but not the firearm type. I get my point across and get the rules enforced just fine without them. I have had to arrest people in the park. Sometimes people in the park don't understand that our rangers here are full-time certified peace officers. We have the same authority to enforce the laws in the same way as state officers, such as highway patrol and local township and city police.

Heroes and Mentors

My father is my biggest hero and mentor. He came from a family of 11 children, down in Kentucky. A Black male in southern Kentucky, it don't get much more remote than that. Growing up, he was an athlete, and his team could only play other Black schools in the area. Being in the South was tough. He went into the military too. He would tell me about being in the Service and riding on trains. The train might stop in a town, and the Blacks had to go around the back, while the white soldiers would go in the front door of the diner and have the best of everything.

Just thinking about all the stuff my father had to go through, and looking back on it now, I have a deeper respect for him. Knowing what my father went through as a kid, and what he gave up to go into the Service so he could send money back home to his mom to help the family, is incredible.

This was a man who could have gone on and played college and professional basketball, because he was extremely talented. He was known in the tri-state area of Ohio, Kentucky, and Indiana as one of the best players

In these places you can forget about your problems for just a small moment while you are there. When you get back to the daily grind, of course, you find they are still there, but for that moment, 5 minutes or 5 hours, however long you were there, those problems in your life seem to have vanished.

around. Everybody knew my dad. He played against Oscar Robertson. He went into the Air Force and gave up a basketball career in college to support his family. He went on to play for the all-Air Force team. You have to be the best of the best to play on that team.

I look at opportunities now and think about my dad and how would he handle things. If I have a situation that arises on my job that is bugging me, then I can go talk to my father. I have friends that are great people, super smart, good listeners, but it is not the same as sitting down with your dad and getting advice.

You know, I hear kids today talking about Michael Jordan and all his fame and fortune. I think that is great, it is good he is doing so well, but if that is what defines a personal hero for you, then I think you need to look a lot harder.

The Spirit and Nature

Being outdoors for me is very spiritual. I am not a church-going person anymore. Nature is my way of connecting with God. Just getting far enough from town to be able to stand there and just listen to all the birds, or just the wind going through the trees, or whatever. Being able to sit on a cliff and watch the sunset or sunrise—I cannot imagine anything more spiritual or beautiful than that.

I think that is one of the reasons I am so into the outdoors, because it gives me such a sense of satisfaction actually being able to see the hand of God, knowing that he created this. He has given people the knowledge to protect these places. In these places you can forget about your problems for just a small moment while you are there. When you get back to the daily grind, of course, you find they are still there, but for that moment, 5 minutes or 5 hours, however long you were there, those problems in your life seem to have vanished. Being out there focuses you.

I could be sitting here in the office doing reviews or something, and realize I need a break. Come on now, I work in a park, so I can walk right out the door and across the road and just stand there and relax and gather myself. I may just stand and watch a red-tailed hawk sitting in a tree, and it just flies by me, and I just stand there and watch it. Now I am focused, and I can go back in and take care of that paperwork.

I have my own connection with God, and I do not need to be in church. My church is the outdoors, which can be anywhere I choose to be.

Youth and Wilderness

When I got out of the Army, I realized I really enjoyed the outdoors, so I went and worked with Big Brothers and Big Sisters at their summer camps, and I had lots of fun showing kids all the cool stuff along hikes, helping inner-city kids experience the outdoors. That was a joy for me, because many of those city kids had never seen a lot of nature and I could show them and say, "Check it out!" And they were happy to learn all the cool outdoor stuff

A doe walks through an urban city park.

I showed them. I thought maybe, just maybe, a kid would enjoy it enough to think, "Hey, maybe this what I want to do for a career—be outdoors."

I do a lot of mentoring now as an adult. I usually have a couple of young guys I take out and talk with from time to time. Most of them are people my mother knows. These are mostly single Black mothers with sons. Most of these guys don't have a male role model in the home, or at least a good role model, so my mom sends them my way. Some of these guys might have gotten into trouble for the first time recently, so their mother gets a hold of my mom and she says, "Hey, let's go over and talk to Marshall."

Milky Way in a Wyoming night sky

I have led a lot of church youth groups, and one of the schools down in my old part of the district requests me every year to come back and talk to their fourth and fifth graders about getting into this field of work. I hope that kids might come back to me and say, "Hey, you inspired me. You came to our school and probably don't even remember me, but you came and talked about how you went from being a full-time ranger within a year to being assistant manager and running your own park, and that inspired me to be something more. You challenged my thoughts of wanting to be a pro athlete, saying, 'What if that does not work out for you, then what?' You gave me the stats that one in 3,000 people ever make it to the NBA. You told me I needed something to fall back on, and you inspired me that day, and now I want to thank you." That is why I enjoy mentoring kids and going into schools and talking to classes.

Best Outdoor Experiences and Favorite Places

I tell you, I ain't even gonna lie, my favorite outdoor activity is golf. It's all about golf! It is the best of both worlds; you got the sports part, you are getting some exercise, and then there is the mental aspect. We were down in Myrtle Beach, my wife and I and another couple, and we were golfing, and I saw some of the most beautiful woodpeckers and warblers and a different finch that I had never seen in Ohio. Really, where else would you see that, unless you go birding in some type of sanctuary? Golf rolls it all up into one great package. I mean, some places I have been, you stand there on those tees and you have forest on one side and ocean on the other, and you say, "Man, God did a great job. This is beautiful. He gave man the knowledge to create such a serene scene in which to calm people so they can hit this shot."

Marshall is now a park manager at Three Creeks Metro Park within the Columbus and Franklin County Metro Park system in Columbus, Ohio. Marshall's career spans 17 years. The Metro Parks system has expanded since I lived there. They provide outdoor recreational opportunities for residents throughout the central Ohio area. I am sure Marshall's face is a welcoming sight to many of the visitors of color using the Columbus-area metro parks.

—Dudley Edmondson

BEING A WIFE AND A GREAT mother has been a life goal for me and comes before my job as a wildlife biologist with the U.S. Geological Survey. I take my children to the outdoors because it is the last vestige of naturalness anymore, it is the last vestige of calmness, it is the last place that they can go and really understand what God has given them in creation.

The way that I experience things now is through experiences with my family; they are no longer just personal experiences. My husband and I can take the time to go out and go camping, or we could spend a day in Utah's Canyonlands National Park over a weekend and do those types of things together. We are looking forward to doing those kinds of things with the girls.

Childhood Experiences and Turning Points in Nature

I was an Air Force brat. We moved around quite a bit. We lived in Florida, then we moved to New Mexico, then we moved to Virginia. We moved to Columbia, South Carolina, when I was 7, so I grew up there and I graduated from high school there. My parents still live there.

I have always been interested in nature on an analytical level, but I was not interested in getting dirty or climbing trees or rolling around in the grass—I was not a tomboy. I was supposed to be a clean little girl and sit down and be pretty; that is the way I was raised. I was allergic to everything, so I could not go out in certain seasons. I could not pick flowers or roll in the grass.

It was not until I went to college that I picked it up again. I wanted to know more. I was more intrigued by the learning element of natural resources versus the actual physical element of it, and then once I learned it, I wanted to see it and

PHADREA PONDS

**Wildlife Biologist, U.S. Geological Survey
Fort Collins, Colorado**

touch it. Once I learned about the anatomy and physiology of a particular bird, I really wanted to find that bird. For me, that was completing the circle. Once I learned about a plant species, I wanted to go out and find that plant.

What I Do in the Outdoors

I specialize in human dimension research. I look at a natural resource or wildlife management policy and I try to figure out how that policy affects or is affected by human involvement. If people live in an area or are recreating in the area, I look at how their activities or involvement in that area affect the land or wildlife habitat.

I study data collected by surveying the public or holding public meetings and focus groups. A lot of people think they can use the land any way they want because it is public land. We try to let them know that yes, they can use the land because it is their natural heritage, but recognize that the wildlife uses the land as well. We teach them about how to respect it. The U.S. Geological Survey does not implement policy; we review policy. We don't regulate land. We are the research side of land management. That information is then turned over to the Department of the Interior land management agencies for them to use.

When someone says, "So, what do you do?" and I say, "I am a wildlife biologist," the reaction is always "What?!" I say, "Did I mispronounce it in some way?" I find that when a white person asks me that question, their reaction is, "Oh, cool." And if a Black person asks me, their response is, "What?!" They say, "What is that?" or "How did you get into that field?"

The mountains are so huge, I think they can take everything I have to release. I can't release it here in the city environment, because it will bounce back, for lack of a better explanation. But in the mountains it will be absorbed and I can just let it go and leave it there.

Heroes and Mentors

My mentors were two Black professors I had in college who I believe to be visionaries in the field of wildlife management. They were very honest with me about what my path as an African American female in this field would

A calm, slow-moving river flows through a quiet canyon in California.

be like. They told me it would not be easy and that I would have to make my own way. They also reminded me that I would become a role model and to be prepared for that. They told me to always be honest with people regardless of the subject matter. They gave me an ethic about professionalism that I really value, and I take that everywhere I go.

The Spirit and Nature

I consider myself to be a very religious and spiritual woman. I have a strong sense of and faith in God. I believe that God is the creator of all things. So when I am in the mountains, I can feel him in the wind and in the cleanness of the air. I feel his presence. And the ocean with its vastness—I feel like a grain of sand in comparison. Then I think, "I must be a very special person for God to put me here at this time to experience what he has made."

A Blackburnian warbler eyes up insects from a branch.

That is the reason why the ocean and the mountains are special to me. They make me realize my place in the universe. I put myself in perspective with the enormous amount of effort it took to make the ocean—God put that same amount of effort into making me. I have a great sense of duty to fulfill whatever purpose he put me here on Earth for.

The mountain air is very cool—I can think. I can hear myself think, I can sort through things that I can't in the confines of the brick buildings. The mountains are so huge, I think they can take everything I have to release. I can't release it in the city environment, because it will bounce back, for lack of a better explanation. But in the mountains it will be absorbed and I can just let it go and leave it there. That is the spiritual side, that is the rejuvenating, therapeutic part of the mountains and the outdoors—it can totally handle anything I want to take and leave there emotionally.

Minorities in Our Wild Places

I was not into nature as a young adult. Visits to my grandparents' were my only exposure. Part of it goes back to the legacy of African Americans in this country, when we were not welcome at any national park in the 1950s and

1960s and before that, so there was nothing for our parents and grandparents to pass on to us about our natural heritage. At that time, there were still places that had signs stating "no colored allowed" at parks and public beaches. So my parents did not grow up going to national parks. So that was something I was never taught to do. They taught me to go to safe places like Grandma's house for the summer. So for me that is something I have to break for my girls. Every place should be safe for them now in this country. I want them to know they are welcome in national parks and public beaches.

I don't mean to offend anyone, but a small part of the reason African Americans do not spend more time in the out-of-doors is because there are not enough amenities, not enough luxury. This is just my very own personal opinion. For example, people might say, "I don't mind going out there hiking and stuff, but I do not want to get my Timberlands dirty, because I spent 150 bucks on them." Or, "I don't mind going hiking, but when are we going back to the hotel for dinner?" They want the conveniences of society. I think African Americans that do go traveling around the country do so in RVs and don't camp in tents. We want the convenience and comforts of home wherever we go. African Americans have become such urban people, and have been urban for so long, that breaking away from those comforts is a very hard thing to do. We want to be clean and well dressed wherever we may go.

It's more like, "Where are you going to go on vacation? Are you going to Disneyland or the Bahamas?" It is about the event in middle- to upper-income communities. In lower-income communities these would not even be an option. In these communities, it is all about survival. "Are your children being fed? Do you have a roof over your head? Are your children safe?" As your income level rises, these needs are covered, and now you have expendable income. African Americans have been in the lower income levels for a long time, and basic subsistence needs can be hard to meet.

I look at survey data on why people recreate, who will recreate, where they recreate, and when will they recreate. People with advanced degrees will recreate. And when I say recreate, I mean they will go to the Black ski conference, or they will go to organized events. But to plan an outdoor event as a family—I think we do not. When I look at data, I look for the independent and dependent variables. The dependent variables would be income, age, and education. If you are under $50,000 annual income, you are less likely to recreate, because the majority of your income is going toward survival. Even though going out into nature may be one of the freest things we can do—you get in your car, you drive, you park your car, and you get out, and you walk in the woods. For some, even something that simple is just out of their income reach.

Youth and Wilderness

Columbia, South Carolina, is a totally different town than it was when I grew up there, because there are a lot of want-to-be gangbangers and they are bringing in an inner-city attitude. I am not afraid to go back, but I look at these kids and I say, "Who are they?" I am struggling to understand this generation now. Their priorities are different, their motivation is different, their attitudes are different, and their respect levels are different. So when we think about our strategies to recruit these kids into the natural resources professions, all of those strategies have changed. Our generation was eager for any opportunity, knowing that the next step after college was a career. The next step for kids now is, "I just want to make it out of high school."

I did not grow up wanting be a wildlife biologist. It was one of those things—doors started opening for me and I just kind of went through them. It was serendipitous that I got into this field. I am certain that it was because people took an interest in me and helped me to understand what my potential was. I really honestly believe that is the key to helping young African Americans understand this as a career. We have to take a personal interest in young African Americans and let them know that this is something you can do. You don't have to be a wildlife refuge manager, but whatever it is in this world you are interested in, if you connect it to wildlife resource management, you can have a career doing what you want, while at the same time protecting the environment.

My husband, all he was told when he was younger was, "If you want to be successful, you must be rich!" So the way to be rich is to be a lawyer, a doctor, or a pro athlete. "You should be a lawyer, you should be a lawyer!"

I tell students, "You want to be a lawyer? Have you ever thought about environmental policy?" There are plenty of people out there graduating with degrees in political science. By connecting that to something you can sell, like natural resources, you can have a job sooner. "You are interested in medicine? Lyme disease is all over the country, new cases of West Nile disease every day." If you are interested in teaching, connect that to the environment. "Don't think you have to get a job teaching in an elementary school, you can teach at an outdoor education center, you can teach at a museum." I cannot think of any occupation that you can't connect natural resources to. There are plenty of jobs. That is what I tell students at job fairs. I am trying hard to get not just one minority to replace me, but to get 25 people interested in this kind of career.

Best Outdoor Experiences and Favorite Places

I love bird-watching. I was real good at one time—very good. I knew the bird calls and everything. Now I am a bit rusty. I still have a life list; I know what I have and have not seen. Every opportunity I get, I am listening and watching for birds. My favorite bird is the painted bunting.

My first enjoyable outdoor experience was during my days in college at Grambling, and after that it was on dates with my husband before we were

A powerful river flows through a mixed forest in Minnesota.

married. One day he said, "Do you want to go camping?" I said yes, but the truth was I had never been camping before. That was when we were at Oregon State. I could not let him think I did not know how to camp. So I played this game right up to the last second. I had taken all of this stuff. I had a cooler full of food and candles for a candlelight dinner. I was going to cook all of this stuff. And he was like, "Where are you going with all of this stuff?" He said, "No, dear, that is not what we are going to do." I said, "Well, what are we going to do?" So we hiked in and he opened up some trees, and then we walked in farther and he opened up some more trees, and then he said, "I guess we will stop here." I thought, "This is not a campground. This is just a patch in the middle of forest." We made a fire, we put the tent up and slept on the ground. After a few more camping trips, I got used to it and began to enjoy it.

Colorado grassland and mountains

Environmental Advocacy and the Future

There is a separate agenda for people of color with respect to the environment. When you look at the history of race relations in this country, you see that African Americans put so much energy into civil rights issues when many European Americans were concerned about the environment. These issues were separate agendas, and they were created as such, and they have not crossed paths yet. The issues are the same, yes. Environmental issues have to do with environmental justice issues, which are civil rights issues.

In the 1960s, affluent white Americans fought for clean water, clean air, clean and green, green, green. African Americans, on the other hand, during the same period of time, just wanted to be treated like humans and be treated fairly. White Americans had equity in life, so they were free to take up environmental causes. We were fighting for equity in life and we still are. The agenda for Blacks or low-income communities will always be different when it comes to environmental concerns until we reach parity on civil rights issues.

Phadrea changed careers, moving from the United States Geological Survey to the National Park Service in 2021, and she also moved to Maryland. She is now the Information Collection Clearance Officer. She coordinates all social-science-related information gathered from public surveys. It's nice to see she is still working in the conservation and environmental world.

—*Dudley Edmondson*

I RECENTLY GRADUATED FROM OREGON STATE University. I actually wrote my own degree program, which is a Bachelor of Science in natural resources, with an emphasis on cultural dimensions and recreation. I really want to work in some sort of park facility administration. I am looking at a master's program in public administration.

I have been involved in hip-hop music all of my adult life. I have also done a lot of writing, including poetry, throughout my life. My hip-hop pseudo name is "Sun Kissed." They nicknamed me that because I always want to work towards something positive, creating music that makes people feel good but still has intellectual content. Habitat restoration, in the case of my current solo project, is a metaphor for how music had been devoid of the things I needed to make it work for me. That is completely related to my natural resources experience, because that is what I had been doing the whole time, restoring habitat. We need to restore the habitat of hip-hop and what it began as—a voice of the people for political issues for real positive messages, with groups like Public Enemy and others. I hope to be able to reach people about the issues I care about with my music, such as natural resources preservation.

Childhood Experiences and Turning Points in Nature

I spent half of my life in Denver and half of my life up here in Portland, Oregon. I grew up in a neighborhood in Denver where it was about 70% Black, and when I moved up here to Portland I was shocked; it was a big transition to a neighborhood that was less than 10% Black. So my childhood was very different, trying to adjust, struggling with my identity, you know.

ALEX JOHNSON

**Oregon State University Graduate
Portland, Oregon**

I spent most of my time growing up in an inner-city environment. Once I moved to Portland, I spent a lot of time growing up in the natural areas around our neighborhood. There were some natural areas that I used to go out into where I was really intrigued by the greenness of Oregon and the opportunities those areas provided. I spent a lot of time there, just running around in the forest with my friends and my siblings, trying to figure out what was out there.

My oldest brother was the one who actually got me connected with the Forest Park Ivy Removal Project. You could say I grew up with the project. When I started, it was probably only in its third or fourth year of existence, so it was real fresh, and a lot of the youth I grew up with were in the project. They were really a diverse group. We really built the project in a lot of ways. It has been a major part of my upbringing. That is how I first became really interested in nature and the outdoors.

What I Do in the Outdoors

I work with the Forest Park Ivy Removal Project. It is a joint venture between Portland Parks and Recreation and the Friends of Forest Park that employs a diverse group of youth crews to remove invasive ivy plants that are choking off native trees and other native plants. We travel together through the forest using a number of tools to get the job done,

Pacific Northwest old-growth forest, Washington

Portland, Oregon, skyline with Mt. Hood in the background

including machetes, hatchets, and saws. I first started out as a youth crew member with the project in 1996, a year after my brother had worked for the project. I worked my way from a youth crew member during the summers, all the way up working year-round as a crew leader and summer program supervisor.

Heroes and Mentors

I have always wanted to work in the parks department because of the way parks engage young people to get interested in nature. I have learned from my mentors, Sandy and Charles, that youth can benefit from a wilderness experience. They can benefit by simply seeing something they don't see every day when they are on the block or when they are at a shopping mall.

Our director here at the Forest Park Ivy Removal Project, Sandra Diedrich, has been like a second mother to me in terms of my development. She has really been a mentor and hero to me in terms of her involvement with and commitment to justice and civil rights issues, and diversity-building efforts in the development of the program at Forest Park. She has always been committed to making the Forest Park Project youth crews as diverse as possible at all different levels, including class, race, and all kinds of international cultural differences. It has been a learning experience for all those involved, including regular park visitors. Exposing those visitors to diverse youth crews working in the park may help to break down stereotypes.

My other mentor has been Charles Jordan, who was the director of Parks and Recreation here in Portland, Oregon. He was real influential to me because I did not have my father around—he died in the early 1990s. Mr. Jordan really encouraged me to go to school and he always joked with me that he was grooming me to be his replacement as the new director of Parks and Recreation. I hope to be able to live up to his expectations someday. Recently, he was appointed Chairman of the Conservation Fund, where he now oversees a major national environmental organization. I really look up to him as one of the first people of color I knew to achieve such a high level in an environmental organization. You really don't see that on the face of big-name environmental organizations.

I have always looked up to my brother. After my father's death, my brother felt he needed to step up as a father figure. He felt it was now his responsibility to teach me how to become a man. I always looked up to my brother and the things he did, though natural resource issues never really engaged my brother like they did me. Once I got here, to Forest Park, things fell into place.

The Spirit and Nature

I spend time in nature, to put it simply, to get away from the stress of everyday life and to find a little spiritual peace, I guess you could say. I feel recharged when I am out in nature and feel a sense of connectedness with previous and future generations. That connectedness comes from knowing that there are still places that have remained unchanged, and I feel the need to make sure they stay that way for future generations.

Youth and Wilderness

The Forest Park Ivy Removal Project has really been important at providing leadership opportunities for youth. I became the youngest crew leader here, at age 17. I was responsible for keeping 15 more crew members safe and working on the ivy removal areas we were assigned. I even got to take them on a camping trip one night. We had one adult chaperone, but the fact that the director would really trust youth to that extent really empowers you. You are not going to gain any skills if you don't try anything new. Here in Forest Park there is an opportunity to do something that is meaningful instead of just perpetuating the consumer culture in which we live in today.

Just by my association with the Forest Park landscape, I realized there is more that I can do with my life than I had dreamed of before. In communities of color it is very common for middle-class kids to think, "I want to be a doctor" or "I want to be a lawyer." I remember I wanted to be an architect before I came down here to Forest Park. Then I realized the way people interact with the land is really important. My experience working with the youth crews here in Forest Park has been the turning point in my life, the thing that changed me forever. Now I have a natural resources degree because I worked here as a youth crew member and leader.

Sometimes youth of color think environmental issues are just for white folks, you know. It somehow translates in their minds that it is a white people issue, not theirs, but that is not the case. We all live on this planet and at some point we all have to think about it—it affects all of our lives.

I would say to youth of color, "Do not blindly follow the paths mapped out for you," to almost quote the book *Black Boy* by famous Black author Richard Wright. You play a sport because you think that is the only thing you can do to advance yourself in this world. In high school I ran track. I was the 400-meter district champion for the Portland area. Because I ran track, I was recruited to play football. Even my coaches tokenized me because I was one of the few Black players on the team, and I was thinking, "Hey, I might be able to get a scholarship by playing football." They always encouraged me to work towards a sports scholarship. Then I visited a college and saw how Black athletes are treated like trained animals. They don't care about your advancement, your intellect, your personal development. They just want the tuition money and a few title games. I did not want to go down that road. To youth of color I say, "There are a lot more opportunities out there for you than a sports scholarship."

I picked myself up academically in resource issues, and because of my background, a door opened for me. Because there were so few students of color seeking those issues, there were scholarships for me and lots of opportunities. Sometimes you have to be a pioneer and look for places where there are not many people like yourself, turn that around in your favor, and seize that chance to move forward. Unless we pioneer and break into some of these fields of study and sit in the classrooms with white students, then the hatred and ignorance will only be perpetuated, maintaining the barriers to particular fields of study that are traditionally thought of as white-only careers.

African Americans' contributions to this country have been, in many cases, written right out of the history books. For example, some of the first forest rangers in this country were Black Buffalo Soldiers. Look at the history of the West and cowboys. Nearly one-quarter of the cowboys in the romanticized Old West were Black folks, and that is completely written out of the history books. So we have to be there, as youth and as up-and-coming leaders who are people of color, to speak up and say,

Canoeists of Trillium Lake in the shadow of Mt. Hood, Oregon

"Our place is here. We need to be put back in the history books. Tell the stories the way they really happened. You can't leave us out of this discussion." That is why I am so involved in natural resources. I want people to know there is an open door waiting for youth of color in natural resources fields of study.

Best Outdoor Experiences and Favorite Places

In terms of memorable good experiences, I have a favorite place I go camping near Mount Hood here in Oregon. In the past couple of years, I have gone there. It is called Trillium Lake, and I have had experiences there with my family that will stay with me the rest of my life. It feels unreal to see all the trilliums growing there along this lake that is shaped like a trillium. Every moment there was picture perfect. Getting out in nature helps you appreciate life and enjoy every moment of your life to its fullest.

Environmental Advocacy and the Future

I think the issue of environmental justice is one of the major bridges for bringing communities of color into the discussion concerning general environmental issues. People need a healthy place to live, which includes clean air and water. It is a fundamental right each of us has. Communities and big companies should work together to get rid of brownfields and old industrial parks. Look at the disproportionate number of freeways that run through poor neighborhoods where people of color are primarily located. These topics are a definite starting point to try and get minorities to participate in environmental discussions.

Sometimes youth of color think environmental issues are just for white folks, you know. It somehow translates in their minds that it is a white people issue, not theirs, but that is not the case. We all live on this planet and at some point we all have to think about it—it affects all of our lives. While we are not thinking about it in communities of color, things are disproportionately impacting us because we are not paying attention and are being exploited by the majority. At some point we will have to wake up and think about environmental issues and how they relate to us.

Alex has gone on to achieve many amazing things, nationally and internationally. When we met in 2006, he'd just graduated from Oregon State with a Bachelor's in Science and Natural Resources. He's since gone on to become the first Black American Chief of Staff of the U.S. Helsinki Commission.

Alex's career has soared and focused on Foreign Policy and Transatlantic security and protecting democratic institutions in Central Europe. He was the policy advisor to the Organization for Security and Cooperation in Europe from 2007 to 2015 in Vienna, just a few years after we met.

Within the Obama Administration, he served as special counsel within the Department of Defense for Russia-Ukraine Affairs. There is so much more, but I would run out of space writing it all. It's people like Alex who make true change in the world, and I am honored to have met him at the beginning of his career.

—Dudley Edmondson

CURRENTLY, I AM A BACKCOUNTRY RANGER with the National Park Service at Rocky Mountain National Park in Colorado. My job entails issuing permits to any visitor coming into the national park for a backcountry outing. On a typical day I issue, on average, about 20 to 30 backcountry permits, which allow visitors to camp or travel up to seven days or nights within the remote back-country regions of the park during the summer.

Childhood Experiences and Turning Points in Nature

I really did not have as much exposure as most people do to the outdoors until my late twenties. I grew up in the Fifth Ward neighborhood of Houston, Texas, with 14 brothers and sisters. It is one of the most socioeconomically disadvantaged neighborhoods in the entire Houston metropolitan area. Fortunately, my educational pursuits have allowed me to experience life outside northwest Houston.

In 1997, I graduated from Eisenhower High in the top 10% of my class. I decided to go to Lady of the Lake University, a small private school in San Antonio. People laugh at me when I tell them that even in the midst of taking 29 hours of master's level course work, I still felt incredibly bored. I felt as though I still had not reached my full potential. If accepted, I am planning to attend Yale University to finish my course work.

One year, when I was 14, my aunt packed us all up and took us to Yellowstone National Park in her RV. We spent about 24 days out there. We would day hike in the park and meet some of the rangers and they would give us talks about the park. I had a blast! I had never seen anything like that in my life. I was used to small houses, shootings on street corners, you know, the drug deals

BRIAN GILBERT

Backcountry Ranger
Rocky Mountain National Park, Colorado

Above the tree line in Rocky Mountain National Park

you would see on the street corners almost daily. Then getting into places like the national parks where you don't see any of that, it kind of just throws you for a loop. You look down a canyon and 500 feet below you there's running water. You ask, "How did it get that way?" When a ranger explains to you about how shifts and geological cracks and water erosion worked together to form the canyon—it really amazed me. Being the bookworm that I am, I jumped into the subject matter and was hooked on it. It was then that I began to realize I had to broaden my horizons; I had to get away from the Houston area and the Fifth Ward.

I am a city slicker for sure. Until this job I had never done any serious backcountry hiking in my entire life. It was an absolutely wonderful experience. I have never tent camped before, so I hope to do that many times before I leave the park this summer. I feel so incredibly honored just to look out this front window of my residence here in the park every day and see Long's Peak standing more than 14,250 feet in the air. I think to myself,

"Wow, this is something only God could create. And I am truly honored to be here."

What I Do in the Outdoors

When I am out there in the backcountry as a ranger on my official hike day, I have people coming up to me asking questions. I find myself perhaps overpreparing for these encounters, knowing that eventually someone will ask me a question, and when they do I will have to answer the question knowledgeably and factually. I can't help but wonder sometimes if their questioning and curiosity is perhaps because they have never seen an African American in the backcountry or in park uniform before.

I read ravenously. I have books and magazines around here everywhere. I am constantly reading. The more I know, the more I can help visitors to the backcountry better enjoy their experience.

I have attended the National Hispanic Environmental Conference and a few other events put on by the Congressional Hispanic Caucus and the Congressional Black Caucus. That's how I made the contact that got me this job. The Environmental Protection Agency, the National Forest Service, and the National Park Service were all trying to recruit me at the same time. The National Park Service did not give me the impression that they were interested in me because I was African American when they tried to recruit me, but they pointed out that my qualifications were above and beyond average for a person coming into a job like this for the summer, regardless of my race. Because they were able to convince me of that, I decided to come here. I can say without a doubt I do not regret my decision.

Heroes and Mentors

Thurgood Marshall, the first African American appointed to the Supreme Court, stands out in my mind as one of my heroes. I found in some of his writings at the Library of Congress that he was very in tune with the environment. There were a lot of environmentally based cases in the 1970s, beginning with the Brownfield cases of 1971 through 1975. In most of those he kind of went with the majority, finding in favor of the litigants who were suing big companies, mostly dealing with spillage or dumping of toxic waste nearly literally in their own backyards. These were minority inner-city neighborhoods that neither had the legal resources or recourse to do anything about it.

Minorities in Our Wild Places

I would say that the current number of African Americans who participate in outdoor activities is severely underestimated. You really don't hear about, say, your family reunions, where you have 350 family members that might have a reunion on national forestlands and have a big picnic, using the facilities for a week. You do not hear about groups of African American RVers who start in Oregon every year and make their way to Yellowstone National Park in late May.

For the typical African American, I would say they do not spend anywhere near the amount of time that most other ethnic groups do outdoors. Not because of an unwillingness to do so, but because in many cases they do not have the experience to know where to go so they can enjoy themselves, or they don't have access to the resources that would allow them to actually enjoy the outdoors.

. . . I have a personal interest in providing quality-of-life improvements for all Americans for generations to come. I feel compelled to impact the environment in a positive manner.

Best Outdoor Experiences and Favorite Places

I can't say enough that it is such an awesome, spiritual experience when I get out into the backcountry. I drove up the top of Trail Ridge Road here in Rocky Mountain National Park, which peaks at about 13,500 feet. I had never been up that high in a car before. I was so overcome by what I was able to see with my eyes that I have to admit I cried a bit. I was like, "Man, there is no way to describe this." It was just amazing.

I have a journal that I started keeping about five years ago, and when I wrote my entry for the day of my 13-mile hike this week, I found myself overwhelmed and consumed by the experience. I usually start my journal writing at about 10 p.m., and it usually takes me about 35 minutes to enter a day's reflections. However, before I knew it, I discovered it was 2:15 a.m.! I was still writing and had to stop myself. I had so much sensory overload about what had occurred in those six hours when I was out in the backcountry—the sights, the sounds, the scent of flowers all just overwhelmed me. I think this is a period of emotional and spiritual growth for me. It is allowing me to be in an environment where I don't have to focus on anything intellectual or economic; I can just relax and be myself.

If anything, being outdoors gives me the opportunity to learn more about myself. When you get out there away from people, where you do not hear anything except maybe water in a river or the wind whistling through the trees, you develop such clarity in your thoughts. Anything you are worried about or obsessing over becomes clearer in your mind—you become much more proactive and you come up with solutions where you thought there were none.

Being a Face of Color in Remote Places

I would not say I have experienced racial prejudice in the outdoors overtly, but more covertly. People consider me to be a token of some sort. They see me as a young African American in a high-paying job. I actually earned my position here and did not get it from some affirmative action mandate or

A stunning view of the continental divide west of Denver, Colorado

other quota and set-aside program to provide people of color with quicker access to government jobs. People need to get that kind of crap out of their minds. All they would need to do is have a conversation with me and they would see I was more than qualified to do this job. The fact that I am African American is just a coincidental benefit.

Bull elk standing in a meadow in Colorado

Environmental Advocacy and the Future

A lot of people don't understand why I am so adamant about environmental issues at such a young age. I tell them I have a personal interest in providing quality-of-life improvements for all Americans for generations to come. I feel compelled to impact the environment in a positive manner. One day I would like to be able to go to a national park like Rocky Mountain or the Grand Canyon or to a national monument anywhere in the United States with my wife and children, once I am married and settled, and be able to enjoy the same pristine environment that I am enjoying now as an employee of the National Park Service. I am fascinated by the thought of seeing my life come full circle from a patron of the parks today, to the other side as a bureaucratic administrator charged with natural resource protection tomorrow.

When I was on the speech-and-debate team during high school, I was amazed by the number of environmental issues that we ran across. It exposed me to a lot of different writers, particularly Rachel Carson and her book *Silent Spring*. I read that for the first time in 1995, when I was a sophomore in high school, and it changed my entire worldview. Before that, I was the type of kid who would ride his bike down the street and throw a soda can into the gutter. After reading that book, I suddenly became an "environmental nut," to quote my mother. I would gather up recycling and take it to the center. I would recycle plastic, cardboard, and cans. Soon my entire immediate family got involved in recycling and became more environmentally conscious. I keep them up to date on environmental issues so they know what is going on around the country. Currently, I am interested in the US stance on the Kyoto protocol and the reduction of greenhouse gas emissions by the world's most industrialized nations.

I feel that I have a place and a particular purpose here on Earth. I will contribute to environmental preservation and do my part just like any other human should who has a passion for the environment and understands how important it is to preserve it.

Brian has completely changed careers and is now an accountant with Intermodal Tank Transportation, Inc., at their Houston, Texas, offices, which is also his hometown. At the time we met, he was young and new to the National Park Service. He seemed really excited about his work and looked forward to serving and educating the public. I think he made a great role model for young BIPOC visitors to the park.

—*Dudley Edmondson*

AUDREY: AS AN IMMIGRANT FROM JAMAICA, I had never heard of the national park system. I had lived in the US for 15 years prior to our marriage, in New York and Florida, but had never heard of the national parks. Of course, I had heard of the Grand Canyon and Yellowstone, but they had no relationship to my life at the time, because they were nowhere I thought I would ever go. When Frank and I got married in 1992, he shared this desire he had for us to travel around the country and discover America through the national parks. My God, that started us on the greatest adventure of our lives, and ultimately took us to where we are today, as people deeply involved in conservation. I would suggest that every breath we breathe that is not given to each other, or our children, or our friends is really given to the conservation of the natural world.

FRANK: I think one of the moments of clarity for me about what it means to have a tradition in your family to protect these places came at Yellowstone. I was there near the lodge and I pointed to an area on the building that looked like it had been scorched by fire. I said, "I wonder if that is where the fire was in 1988?" A gentleman standing near me, a white gentleman from Chicago, just happened to overhear me, and he said, "Yes, that is where the fire was because when I brought my son, they had just finished rebuilding that section, and when my father brought me, they had just finished building that section." His father had brought him, and he had brought his son, and now he was coming back to visit after retiring from his job. That was the first time the idea of ownership hit me. Here three generations of people had visited that park, they owned that park, they feel that is their park! We

FRANK & AUDREY PETERMAN

Conservationists
Atlanta, Georgia

Frank and Audrey on the shores of Lake McDonald
in Glacier National Park, West Glacier, Montana

have not been able to instill that sense of ownership in African American families in any major way. There are a number of reasons for that, but it made me realize that I had not done that for my sons and my daughters.

Childhood Experiences and Turning Points in Nature

AUDREY: I grew up in Jamaica, in that little village everybody talks about—that "it takes a village to raise a child." It was the kind of place where everybody knew everybody from three to four generations back. The biggest excitement for us as children was to wake up early on Saturday morning and a group of kids would decide to go to the mango bushes, which stretch out for acres and acres, and we would have a little basket on our heads and find these big fat ripe mangos lying on the ground. There was a little stream running just below our property where I would spend a lot of time observing

An entrance sign to Glacier National Park

the fish and being tranquilized by the water. A love for nature was certainly nurtured in the environment where I grew up, because we got our food from the backyard. You know, the meat from chickens running around in the yard. Or kill a pig from the pen in the backyard. We lived very close to nature in my homeland.

FRANK: I grew up outdoors. I grew up in southern Florida, when it was still possible to go out after school in the summertime and stay outdoors until sundown, and eat mangos and other wild fruits that were growing. I learned how to swim in the canals, and played baseball with Seminole Indians.

I was born in Alabama. Some of my earliest experiences in the outdoors were following my grandfather through the woods as a little boy. In Native American culture, I guess you would call him a shaman because he knew all of the roots and plants and their healing properties. Not in a voodoo or occult sense, but in a real medicinal sense. I really do not recognize any period in my life where I did not feel connected to nature.

My father worked in the orange groves in Florida. That was when the orange groves were still full of wildlife. You could see rattlesnakes, foxes, and otters. So all of my life I was always near nature. I had no idea at the time that it needed to be protected. I just thought everybody felt the same way I did about the outdoors. I did see it being cut down all around me, but it did not register at the time that this was really ending a way of life I had always known.

My earliest experience of recognizing the damage that could be done to nature was probably in the first or second grade. Our school was in this old building that had huge windows that you could really see out of really well. There was a huge old ficus tree, or rubber tree as we called it, and it spread out over half an acre, I would guess. We played in this tree during recess a lot. I looked out those windows one day and they were cutting this old tree down. What was so interesting about it was that it was right near the time that we had a lesson about the oxygen exchange and how important plants were to that. So I am looking out there at this tree being cut down, and I am almost not able to catch my breath from shock, as though cutting this tree down was choking off my breath. It was at that point in my life when I realized the effect man's activity could have on the environment. No one satisfactorily explained to me why the tree had to be cut down. It made a tremendous impression on me at the time.

What I Do in the Outdoors

FRANK: Presently, I am Regional Public and Political Awareness Director for the Wilderness Society for the East Coast, which is from the state of Maine to Florida. I try to figure out ways to actually build a constituency in the African American community to support wilderness conservation and land protection. That is job number one! We have begun to work with historically black colleges and universities, which are the land grant colleges that were set up right after slavery ended for African Americans. We are working principally in North Carolina, because we have forest management plans coming up, so we want to begin to educate the populace there about how they can participate in helping to shape those plans and what it means to their lives. I also work a great deal with the Congressional Black Caucus, and we have gotten Congressman John Lewis of Georgia to agree to have a brain trust on land conservation at their annual meeting. That is exciting because normally when you get an issue elevated to brain trust status, it picks up media attention and the issue then gets a higher profile. We are trying to show the African American community the connections between their health and welfare and the protection of these very special wild places.

AUDREY: I'm the manager of our website, earthwiseproductionsinc.com, and I publish the newsletter *Pick up & GO!* It is a bimonthly newsletter that focuses on the environment and travel to the national parks. The idea being that if we show people of color the existence of these beautiful places first of all, then we show them that there is Black history in these places that is not widely known, we might get their attention. We also show them the connection to the larger environmental debate and how it affects their lives, both in terms of the conservation of green spaces and in terms of the pollution

A fall view of the Tetons in Glacier National Park

in the cities, and how their actions can affect both of those issues. I also do speaking engagements, and I serve on a couple of boards, which is one of the reasons why we are here in Glacier National Park today, as part of the board of the National Parks Conservation Association. That organization helps chart the future of the National Park Service, and we are both a close ally and critic of the National Park Service. My really big focus serving on this board is promoting the issue of diversity and outreach to communities of color. Unfortunately, there is still a big perception in the white community that people of color are not interested in the environment or are too poor to participate; it is very bizarre, I think.

Heroes and Mentors

FRANK: The most influential people, my heroes and mentors in life as a kid, were, no doubt, my father and grandfather. My grandfather was half Creek Indian, so almost from birth I had this connection, this reverence towards nature, because I was taken into the woods and shown sassafras tea and things like that. My grandfather instilled in me at a very early age that I was a part of all of this, that I was part of nature, that I was just one more element in this wonderful fabric we call the natural world.

My father insisted that on all the groves that he managed, the owner had to set aside a portion of the grove that would remain unharvested, and that was the deal he made before he would take it over. He said that was a Biblical injunction that you're supposed to set aside a portion of whatever you farm for the animals and wildlife.

AUDREY: If I were to speak of people who inspired me as mentors and heroes when I was growing up, it would be my whole neighborhood, my whole village, because everybody lived so close to nature, and we were respectful of nature, and we were respectful of each other. One of the odd things I find now is that all these people who are promoting the protection of nature don't seem to care about people. To me, that is incomplete. It is out of balance.

The Spirit and Nature

AUDREY: I have a very spiritual connection to nature. This is what drives me. I am not a church-going person, we are not church people. We celebrate God in the face of God, as we see it every day where we are, outdoors. Frank and I take walks in the mornings near our home in Atlanta, and the cars are whizzing by us, but we are looking at the birds or saying, "Oh, what kind of bird is that? What kind of plant is that?" This kind of experience gives life such an enriching, exciting quality. That is what we want to share with other people. Just pay attention to the natural world around you. The show that nature is putting on for you is such a dazzling performance all the time, if you will just tune in to see it.

Minorities in Our Wild Places

AUDREY: Some of the most interesting and enjoyable things we have done include lobbying Congress to help get the Selma to Montgomery National Historic Trail in Alabama. We helped to get that legislation passed. We helped to get legislation passed for the National Underground Railroad Network to Freedom passed. I feel as though African Americans have never felt a sense of ownership about this country. It is like we are tenants in this country. When you go out and visit the national parks, and you show somebody, and you say, "Hey, this belongs to you. Your tax dollars pay for this. It is part of your natural heritage." Then you tell them about their ancestors who were there as enslaved Africans, who found their freedom going through the Everglades on to places like the Bahamas, etc., or that Colonel Charles Young and the Buffalo Soldiers were the ones who protected the giant sequoias in 1903, then African Americans begin to see themselves reflected in the fabric of the country in ways that the history books don't show them.

FRANK: The green community and the government organizations, like the National Park Service and the Agricultural Department and the Department of the Interior, will really have to make a general appeal in regards to information and education distribution to minority communities. Now they all cry they don't have the money to do that. My answer is you can't afford not to do it. Because if you don't do it, if you let the protection of these places continue to be perceived by minorities as being places of privilege for the elite, then minority groups are not going to care about it, and when they become the majority, they will strike them down. The work you do today in conservation will have very little meaning tomorrow if you don't embrace the up-and-coming majority; it is unsustainable. Even when you get a green organization with diversity programs in their budgets, it is the first thing cut, first thing. To me it should be at the top of their list for funding. A lot of it, I think, is a kind of unspoken, unexpressed resistance to doing anything extra for "those people." I think that there are many people on boards, in decision-making capacities, who are not racists and who are not hostile to Black people, but who really resent that you would ask them to spend any money to do anything special to attract this group, because in their minds they think it is their own fault that they are not taking advantage of this resource.

We were completely captivated, and we fell madly in love with the national park system. I think it was somewhere in New Mexico that Frank and I looked at each other and said, "Where are the Black people out here?" Among the hundreds of thousands of white people and Japanese people we were seeing, we saw just two Black people in the 14 national parks we visited, traveling north to south, coast to coast, 12,000 miles around the country.

Best Outdoor Experiences and Favorite Places

AUDREY: Frank and I saved up our money for a year, and we bought some camping and hiking equipment. We took off from Florida and drove all the way up the East Coast to Acadia National Park. Camped out for the first time in our lives right there in the park. Then we drove up Cadillac Mountain, where we were above the clouds, and the scenery was so beautiful that it was almost heart-stopping. Then we drove across the middle of the country to visit Yellowstone National Park. To our amazement, we discovered it was not just about one geyser. We learned that, in fact, this was the world's largest concentration of geysers, right there in Yellowstone. From there we drove to the Grand Canyon, which cannot be described. It must be experienced to be believed. Then we continued on to Olympic National Park, where we were able to experience the rainforest on one side of the road, and wade out into the ocean and actually touch sea creatures and starfish on the other side of the road. It was just an incredible, amazing, wonderful experience. Then we drove to the Petrified National Forest, where we saw trees that had turned to stone over millions of years, and they were glowing like 40-ton jewels.

The year was 1995, and we traveled from August to October. We were completely captivated, and we fell madly in love with the national park system. I think it was somewhere in New Mexico that Frank and I looked

An impressive number of turkey vultures fly high over the Grand Canyon in Arizona.

at each other and said, "Where are the Black people out here?" Among the hundreds of thousands of white people and Japanese people we were seeing, we saw just two Black people in the 14 national parks we visited, traveling north to south, coast to coast, 12,000 miles around the country.

Being a Face of Color in Remote Places

FRANK: It is hard for white people who have not experienced the generations of discrimination to understand the impact that it has had on a whole group of people. African Americans are still fearful of hostilities they may be met with in those areas of the country that are still principally white. The environmental and conservation movement is primarily white. We (Black people) have an aversion to being in remote areas, because this country has a history of being racist, and we don't want to expose ourselves to hostility or abuse. Therefore, if you want minorities to participate, especially African Americans, then you are going to have to roll out the welcome mat, and you are going to have to tell them things have changed, and you will have to let them know they are wanted and needed. The number one reason minorities give for not traveling to these places like Audrey and I had done, was they were physically afraid of going out there and being accosted by racist whites. That was the number one reason from both Blacks and Hispanic groups! If you look back at all the pictures of the lynching of Blacks in this country, they are always out in the woods, in a tree somewhere. That weighs very heavy in the minds of African Americans. You have to figure ways to help overcome these fears and reservations about being in the outdoors among minorities. You do need a massive program. You can't just say, "Oh, well, gee, eventually they will get the message that it is OK for them to be out here!" It is just not going to happen that way.

AUDREY: You know, we have never experienced racial prejudice in the outdoors. Since we took our trip around the country in 1995, we have really done nothing else but be involved with the outdoors, and still have had no incidents of racial prejudice. We have gone to places where people have given us some funny looks. We rode into Gillette, Wyoming, one evening just before dusk, and Frank wanted a beer, so we went to the local store and they said, "You have to go to the bar if you want alcohol." So we walked to the bar and we opened the door, and I swear to God—and we still joke about this—even the jukebox skipped a beat! It was like time stopped in the place, and every head turned and looked at us. But, hey, we are citizens of the world, and this country is as much ours as it is anybody's, so we walked up to the bar, and the young woman was very friendly, and we got our beer and we left, and everything went back to normal.

Then one day we had the opposite experience, and it is one I will treasure forever. We pulled into Zion National Park on our trip around the country, and we had gotten in pretty late, so we turned in right away. The next morning we got in the truck because we wanted to drive around and see the park. We were in awe of the place. We were coming back to camp and we see this young white girl hitchhiking with her thumb out. It was very early on a Sunday morning, around 7 a.m., so we stopped and picked her up. Sure enough, she hopped into the truck, not even giving it a second thought, as though we had known each other all our lives. Turned out that she and her boyfriend were going on a multiday hike and she had dropped the car off on one end while he had gone ahead with their gear up to the trailhead. Funny thing is that we could not stop laughing and talking about how we were probably the only Black people in the surrounding four states. So we were joking that, imagine her surprise and luck, that a truck pulls up and there are Black people inside. To her it was not big deal. She was so nice and friendly, and race was not a big deal to her.

We have found that, in most cases, it is a much friendlier country than it is pictured to be on TV, really. When we were camping in Acadia National Park, our first night in Blackwood's campground—oh, my God, the family that was in the site next to us were so friendly, they would not leave us alone. Before they left the next day, they brought all their firewood over for us to use. They really were trying to make us feel very comfortable and welcomed. That is really what our experience has been like consistently in the outdoors.

Environmental Advocacy and the Future

FRANK: We are constantly faced with the question, both from congressmen and from leaders in the community, "Is this a real priority for these communities? These communities are concerned with crime and other issues." One of the challenges we have is to frame the protection and conservation issues in such a way that is not seen as competing with issues of environmental justice. Unfortunately, there has been some tension between the green community and the environmental justice community. And that tension is well deserved, in terms of the green community seeming to not have embraced this issue of environmental justice in a meaningful way. This, of course, sort of angers the members of the environmental justice groups who feel they are dealing with life-and-death issues, such as the EPA's National Priority list sites, that have direct health effects on people. We want to make sure that we embrace the thought that there is a relationship between land protection and the great outdoors, and the environment in the inner city and urban areas, and that is a challenge.

Population demographics drive some of the concern today about the future of conservation and protection. You're probably going to have, proportionately, more elected Black officials from Virginia to Florida than anywhere in the US. Most land use is local. The Florida Everglades disappeared on Tuesday and Thursday nights, when the city and county councils met and passed the zoning ordinances. It did not disappear by acts of Congress; it disappeared by what happened in city council meetings. That means you are getting more and more Black people who are making decisions about the use of the resources at the local level. Therefore, we must begin making that connection between the decisions they make and what it does to conserve and protect natural areas. That it is not a matter of using that resource up to offset some tax credit, but it is about preserving that resource that can benefit their children.

AUDREY: The great outdoors does not belong to any particular group of people. It is there for all Americans to enjoy, and you can all take from it lavishly. The conservation of the natural world is going to be the most important issue facing the next generation, because already we have altered the landscape to the point where we are reaping what we have sown. We have fouled our air and our water and our land, and it is having repercussions on our health. The most important thing you can do is to recognize that you have a connection to the earth. Food comes from the earth. The air that you breathe is important. The water that you drink is important. It is not guaranteed to be there forever. Understand that when it goes, so do humans, including you, because these are building blocks of your life.

I've always thought of them both as the catalysts responsible for helping Black Americans embrace our National Park System. Frank and Audrey have been on this mission for so many decades and are still making an impact on that front. They've moved back to Audrey's homeland of Jamaica but still come to the States to do this important work of helping Black Americans understand and explore their natural heritage, which is our public lands system.

—Dudley Edmondson

THE LAUGHTER AND ACTIVITIES OF CHILDREN

seemed to bring to life the working-class neighborhood where I grew up in Columbus, Ohio.
I remember it being full of kids of very similar
ages, and many of the boys played street football
together. Man, that was the best way to spend a
summer afternoon. I feel very fortunate that my
family spent a lot of time with extended family
members, which included aunts, uncles, cousins,
and my grandparents. Kids had so much adult
supervision then from people they knew, trusted,
and loved; it worked really well.

I was unfortunate, however, to have been
drawn to nature as a direct result of my father's
alcoholism. As a little boy, I collected insects
and bred tropical fish. It was my way of bringing
nature, my quiet safe haven, into the house and
allowing me to escape the emotional turmoil and
dysfunction of my home environment. My dad
had a very limited education and struggled with
expressing himself as he was handicapped by a
very severe stuttering problem and an equally
severe hearing loss, causing him great emotional
and psychological pain. Sadly, alcohol became
his escape device from his own flesh-and-bone
prison. I did not understand that until I moved
away. I have forgiven him for it; life is just too
short to harbor such corrosive thoughts in one's
mind. Today I have nothing but love in my heart
for the man.

I honestly had never even thought about how
nature became such an important part of my
life until I started writing this book. I guess it
has been there for so long, I'd just blocked out
the traumatic circumstances under which it had
gotten there in the first place. Sometimes bad
experiences cause us to discard all memories of

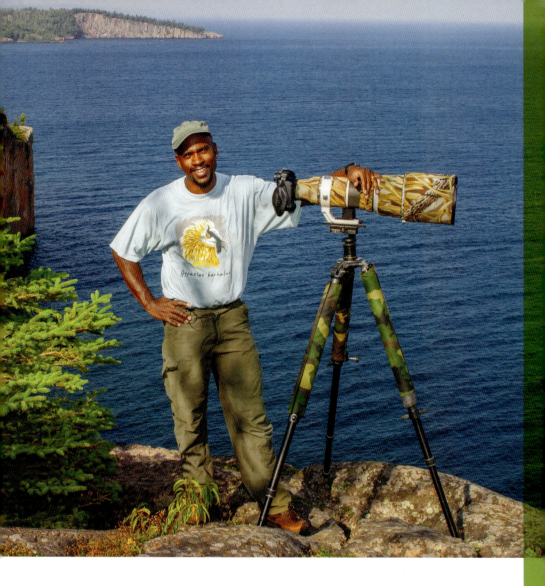

DUDLEY EDMONDSON

**Professional Nature Photographer and Writer
Duluth, Minnesota**

everything that happened during periods of time in our lives. Sometimes you must go back and do a search-and-recovery mission, sifting through the ruins to find the lost treasures in order to get closure in your life. For me, the shiny artifact discovered among the rubble is my love for nature.

Childhood Experiences and Turning Points in Nature

I first got into nature on weekend family picnics at a place called Hoover Dam on the outskirts of Columbus. My mother would make us food on the grill, bringing boiled potatoes, hot dogs, hamburgers, and coleslaw. Mom would slice up the boiled potatoes, mix them with chopped onions, a little salt, pepper, and Crisco, and make home fries in a cast-iron skillet. As kids we got to see nature up close and personal in the woods around the reservoir. I was free to go exploring in the woods on my own, as long as I stayed within earshot of my parents. My parents were not outdoor people. They just liked getting away from the noise and heat of the big city.

Some kids teased me about being a "nature bug." They called me Euell Gibbons, the one-time pitchman for Grape Nuts cereal. When they would see me doing something kind of "woodsy," they would always quote one of his lines from the commercials, "Did you know many parts of a tree are edible?" and then they would laugh at me. It bugged me, but I got over it.

What I Do in the Outdoors

In 1989, I moved north, to Minnesota, looking for a fresh start and a career as a nature photographer. I did not really have a plan for how I was going to go about it, just the desire to make it happen. When I think back on it today, I think one of the reasons it worked was that it never occurred to me that I couldn't do it. I followed leads, read books and magazines on nature photography, and just stuck with it.

About eight years ago, all my efforts paid off when I got a call from Stan Tekiela, a local author who was looking for photos of birds for a field guide he was writing. His guide really sold well, and he began branching out into regional, then national guides covering common flora and fauna. We started traveling nationwide, shooting on location from Alaska to Florida and every state in between. We learned to work quickly and efficiently. Some days we felt like hired guns. We'd blow into town, check in at the hotel, flop our camera bags out on the beds, load both camera bodies with film, pack a photo vest full of lenses and extra film, grab our tripods, and hit the door in hot pursuit. We would assess a situation and quickly determine what we needed to do to get the image. We often had it figured out within a half a day or by the end of our first day on location, which is rare. We became a serious photographic duo and always got publication-quality images of the species we were after.

To show up to photograph several species of birds that you have never worked with before and walk away with full-frame killer shots of them just does not happen often, but he and I did it consistently. It is typically a real waiting game, but we figured out ways to get around it. We would also build our own outdoor studio on-site when needed. We developed a way to photograph reptiles, amphibians, and small mammals without harming them or removing them from their habitats. We'd set up a small enclosure around the animal and maybe add some leaves, a rock, or a piece of log. Once we got the shots we wanted, we took down the enclosure and returned the natural elements to their places. Sometimes these studio setups would require a few extra bits and pieces, so we both carried spring clamps, duct tape, wood scraps, and cordless power tools in our SUVs, just in case. Some of the shots we got of elusive species were incredible.

. . . I can just get caught up in the moment of enjoying whatever natural beauty I find around me. It is very peaceful to me, like a form of meditation.

I found that photographing wildlife takes a lot of patience. I would say it might be the single most important component of the job. You have to study their behavior and determine the best time and location to get a publication-quality image. Learning predictable patterns like migration routes or nesting behavior gives you a slight, but large enough, advantage to achieve your objective. Over the years I have been both successful and totally skunked, but you never give up. Lusting after that perfect image keeps you on the hunt with a feeling that, any moment, all your effort could pay off.

A few years ago, I walked away from that very lucrative career and called it quits, looking for a new challenge, wanting to branch out and do my own books and return to more artistic and creative photographic work. I have a lot of good memories and tens of thousands of great images from those

Natural Bridges State Park in California

days in my stock files that I still market for publication. I am certainly a better photographer from the experience.

Today I am slowly remolding myself, adding outdoor adventure photography to my repertoire, chasing down mountain climbers, kayakers, and extreme sports enthusiasts of all types. Specifically, I've been looking for African Americans and other people of color in these activities, in an effort to create images that could change the way people of color see themselves and maybe, in the process, also change the way America sees them. In this country, African Americans and other minorities are often seen or referred to as a group, rather than as individuals, and that bugs me. The danger is that individuals in these groups lose their identities in the collective consciousness of society. Flesh-and-blood people are transformed into statistical data on diagrams and charts showing crime rates, drug use, unemployment, and poverty. When that is allowed to happen, I think society feels a little less compassion for them, even developing a sense of indifference towards the group. I say, "See the individuals—be an individual!"

Heroes and Mentors

As a child, I looked up to my elders, nearly every adult in my life, including neighbors. I did not have any heroes or role models associated with the outdoors, though.

As I got older, my heroic inspiration came from jazz legend Miles Davis. Miles seemed to be a man with no boundaries, and I really admired him for it. Miles was a musical innovator, a shape-shifter of sorts, influencing and molding musical styles like a blacksmith working hot metal. Miles changed the orbit of music like an asteroid slamming into the side of a planet. His innovative genius birthed the landmark recording *Bitches Brew*, the album that started jazz fusion, creating an entirely new genre of music. I admire people who lead and do not follow.

I admire and respect those who've come before me, but also have always been one to follow my gut instinct more than anything else, often choosing to do things my own way. So far, it has not let me down.

The Spirit and Nature

Nature offers more than I can even describe in words. I find that my mind becomes extremely clear when I am outdoors. In that space, I can analyze my thoughts and think them through very thoroughly, or I can just get caught up in the moment of enjoying whatever natural beauty I find around me. It is very peaceful to me, like a form of meditation.

I connect with everything around me—the trees, the plants, and the animals. Kind of like how Neo, the character from *The Matrix* movies, would pick up the ringing phone at the end of a hallway to pass through a portal back to the real world. Every living creature in the outdoors is a portal to me between our world and the real world, each one offering a quick escape from the fast-paced, stressful, man-made consumer culture we live in. That portal could be a ruby-throated hummingbird with its throat patch shimmering like a crown jewel in the sunlight as he sips nectar, moving from flower to flower in your garden.

Or going for a walk alone in the woods on a windless day and admiring snowflakes falling slowly and silently through the pine forest canopy a hundred feet above your head. You look up, stick out your tongue, and catch a single flake right on the tip. Several more land on your glove and, just before they melt, you take notice of their symmetry and unique beauty. The forest is nearly silent except for the sound of your own footsteps and the raven croaking in the distance. In that setting you're drawn into the moment and it is really hard to think about anything else. It is very hard to explain what that feels like to someone who's never experienced it before. It can be an epiphany moment and is really something people should see and feel for themselves.

I am not a church person. I believe in nature and the earth's ability to create life. I also believe in my ability to effect change in my own life. That is not to say that I don't believe in a higher power. I just see no reason to burden myself with trying to answer the question of whether such a power exists. Personally, I rather enjoy dwelling in the mystery of it all, how we got here, and what our purpose on Earth is. To me, it makes being in the outdoors that much more exciting and enjoyable. The mystery component drives me to want to discover more and more about the natural world around me.

Minorities in Our Wild Places

I hear from time to time that we (Black people) don't do this or don't do that, referring to activities uncommonly associated with African Americans,

The buttes of Badlands National Park, the very spot where Dudley first experienced utter silence

many of which involve the outdoors. Every time I hear it, I have to think, "What does this mean?" In particular, what does it mean to the person who said it and, in the larger sense, to African American culture? Does that mean that all Black people are born with this short list of things African Americans are supposed to enjoy in life? African Americans are only supposed to enjoy things in urban settings, not in wilderness settings? Think about how absurd that is—as if outdoor equipment packages had labels that read, "Warning: Not for use by Black people."

In the early 1980s, when I was a teen, I went to visit a good friend one day. I was all excited about a new four-wheel drive pickup I bought. I jumped out of it in his driveway saying, "Check it out!" He and his father walked out of the house, looked at the truck, then looked at me. His father said, "You tryin' to be a white boy, ain't you? Don't you know niggers don't drive 4x4 pickup trucks?" Now this came out of the mouth of a Black man from the South that I viewed as an elder, someone I should look up to. It confused me. I felt ashamed, as though I had done something wrong or that he was somehow right. So where does this concept of what is Black and what is not come from? If you want to be educated, you are trying to be white—that is one I have heard that circulates around in inner-city schools among Black kids. Why would any race of people want to put limitations on themselves? Weren't there enough limitations put on African Americans by the larger society before the civil rights movement for countless lifetimes?

Best Outdoor Experiences and Favorite Places

One of my more memorable experiences in the outdoors was the first time I experienced complete and utter silence in the outdoors. It has happened to me several times since, and it is one of those things that always takes you by surprise; you stop and you say, "Listen, listen," as a smile blooms on your face. I was on my first trip to South Dakota in the mid-to-late 1980s. It was a solo trip to visit Badlands National Park, the first national park I ever visited in the United States. It was a completely different environment than I had ever been in before. I recall walking across the landscape, amazed by nearly everything I saw. I set out across the flatlands, heading towards the base of a set of buttes about a mile away. Once there, I stopped, looked around, and listened intently. The only sound I heard was the muffled thump of my beating heart—that was it. I was outside in broad daylight, sun shining, midday, but in total silence. I looked around again. This time I stuck my fingers in my ears. When I removed them, I could not tell the difference. I thought to myself, "This cannot be possible. No sound at all?" No cars, no planes, no people, no television or radio, no animals, no wind, just complete and utter silence. I was nearly in shock. I just laughed kind of nervously and said, "Wow," in a low, whispering tone. The word barely fell off my bottom lip. I stood there for several minutes, absorbing the quiet, being careful not to move my feet in the dry soil, as I knew it would break the silence. It may have also been one of the first times I really understood and felt the restorative powers of nature. I eventually set up my camera and took some photographs of the buttes before me, on good old Kodachrome 64. The click of the camera shutter broke the silence like a grenade explosion. Viewing that image today still brings me back to that place, where for a moment it seemed as if time stood still.

Being a Face of Color in Remote Places

Racial prejudice is, unfortunately, a fixture of the American landscape, but the circumstances can be very different, with entirely different outcomes, when people find themselves in the outdoors away from the influence and familiarity of the urban environment. A white person and a person of color who meet in a dark alley in a large city will have entirely different feelings towards one another than if the same two people were to cross paths on a nature trail on the backside of a mountain pass. In that environment, all preconceived notions about one another are usually put aside and thoughts of sharing a common experience come to mind. Even offers of assistance or fellowship at one another's campsite might be offered. I can't count the number of times I have been invited back to someone's campsite for a beer or dinner over the years. I have found that 98% of the people you run into in the outdoors are out there for the same reason you are. They are there to enjoy the natural resources and couldn't care less what color you are. I have encountered some racial prejudice in my travels around the nation. Sometimes it has been nothing more than an unwelcoming stare or a silly question by an obviously ignorant person. Only once did I have an incident in which the N-word was used.

I was camping in a state park in western Pennsylvania with a white friend, and we were camped next to a group of men who obviously did not know we were there, at least I want to think they didn't. All of a sudden the N-word just became part of every conversation they were having, followed by laughter. They would say, "I hate niggers, my kids hate niggers—hell, my dog even hates niggers!" After about five minutes of that, I told my friend, "I am going over there and you don't have to come if you don't want to." We walked over there and, with a big sharp axe in my hand, I said, "Listen here, I paid for my campsite just as you did and I will not listen to this sh@! all night, so if you don't like it here, you can go back to wherever the fu*% you came from." They said, "Ah, man, we are sorry. We did not know you were over there. We'll stop it!" I think they may have also been surprised by the fact that my friend was white. So we went back to our campsite and I was fuming. I said to my friend, "That stuff is totally uncalled for!" He said, "I know, man. I am really sorry and embarrassed that you had to hear that." About 10 minutes later, they started up again with the racial slurs and I started back over there, this time to threaten calling the park ranger, but all of a sudden they broke it up, put out their campfire and went to bed. Needless to say, I slept with my axe under my cot that night, just in case.

That is a very rare situation. In 25 years or more of traveling around the country, that was the first and last time that happened. That was early on in my outdoor adventure traveling, but I refused to let anyone keep me from enjoying the outdoors. I pay the same taxes that support and manage these areas, so I had just as much right to be there as they did. Besides, that weekend my friend and I made the best smoked chicken over an open grill that I have ever had.

Environmental Advocacy and the Future

Some people believe nature exists for humans to use as they see fit. I feel humans are no different than any other life form on Earth and we are all dependent on the same ecosystem for our survival. That puts us all in the same boat, doesn't it? Humans are no more capable of survival without a healthy ecosystem than a wolf in the Minnesota wilderness, or an elephant in the jungles of Africa, or a giant sequoia on the western slopes of the Sierra Nevada Mountains. The question is not how we got here or whom we thank for it, but how do we as humans remain here on Earth and how do we better coexist with the other life forms with which we share our world.

My career has changed slightly, as I am now more focused on video production as a cinematographer and author. My work is more centered on people of color, both in the outdoors, and as it relates to social and environmental justice.

I recently published my fourth book, *People the Planet Needs Now,* which gathers the voices of 25 storytellers from around the country whose work focuses on science and environmental and social justice work.

These subjects will always be important to me, but particularly now, as our government continues to try to erase and eradicate people of color from history and the nation's population through educational and immigration reform and the removal of women's reproductive rights. We are projected to soon be a majority in the coming decades, which will reshape power, and for some, that is clearly a scary proposition.

About the Author

Dudley Edmondson has worked for more than 30 years as a photographer, capturing nature and wildlife subjects around the country for natural history publications in the US and Europe. Dudley proudly carries on a family tradition started by his great-grandfather Monteith Vance, a portrait photographer issued a photography license by the state of North Carolina in 1919.

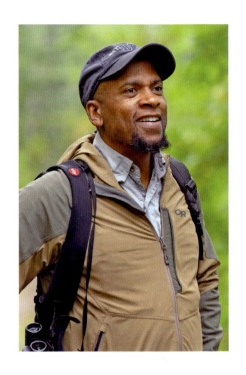

Dudley began work on *Black & Brown Faces in America's Wild Places* in an attempt to find other African Americans around the nation who shared his love for nature and the outdoors. He found several, many of whom he now considers friends. Not until 2005 had he ever been on an outdoor adventure entirely in the company of African Americans; it was a life-affirming experience that he will never forget.

"Nature, without question, is for everyone. It knows no race, creed, or gender and is cheaper than any therapist you could ever hire."

About AdventureKEEN

We are an independent nature and outdoor activity publisher. Our founding dates back more than 40 years, guided then and now by our love of being in the woods and on the water, by our passion for reading and books, and by the sense of wonder and discovery outdoors in beautiful places.

It is our mission to share that wonder and fun with our readers, especially with those who haven't yet experienced all the physical and mental health benefits that nature and outdoor activity can bring. #bewellbeoutdoors